Also by Melisa Torres

PERFECT BALANCE GYMNASTICS SERIES
I've Got This
Nothing Better Than Gym Friends
Dance is the Secret Event
Brothers Have Talent, Too
The Kip
Score Out
Courage to Fly
Season of Change

PERFECT BALANCE GYMNASTICS WORKBOOKS
Goal Setting Journal
Overcoming Mental Blocks
Perfect Balance Gymnastics Coloring Book

Mom and Dad Love Me Series
Mom and Dave Love Me the Same
What if Santa Can't Find Us?

New Challenges

by MELISA TORRES

Copyright © 2021 Melisa Torres
All rights reserved.
Written by Melisa Torres
Cover art by J. Lee and ezarago
Edited by Clara Somers Editing Services
ISBN: 979-848-6172-434

For Bonnie,
Thank you for asking me to feed the kittens in the loft
and for giving me Sassy.

I wish you were here to meet Snowball.

Chapter 1

"What did you decide, Paige?" Trista asks me. We just finished our Level 5 season and my teammates and I are at dinner celebrating our second-place win at our State Meet only hours ago. I surprised everyone, including myself, by staying on beam for the first time all season and scoring a high enough all-around to advance to Level 6. Trista is asking me if I am going to, in fact, move to the Level 6 team.

"I'm not sure yet. I didn't expect to score out today," I answer honestly. She continues to look at me expectantly so I elaborate, "I think I'm just going to see how training goes over the holidays and if I can get my layout on floor."

New Challenges

The thing about gymnastics is that not only do you have to score out of a level to get to the next one, you need to be able to do the harder skills in the next level. I'm so close; I might be ready in January for Level 6. Competition season for Level 5 is in the fall and for Level 6 it's in the winter. So either I move fast and compete Level 6 in six weeks or I wait an entire year. I frown to myself and then add, "Since I'm older, I'd rather not wait until next year." Trista seems to accept this answer and she turns to our teammate Lucy.

"Lucy?" she asks, posing the same question.

"I . . . I'm going to do Level 6," Lucy stammers. "Even if I have to do the back walkover on beam. I'm ready for Level 6," she says. Lucy is the best Level 5 on our team. She is just struggling with her back handspring on beam, which is a Level 6 skill. Technically, it's a nice to have Level 6 skill.

Level 6 is a big change because we get to create our own routines. We will have certain requirements we need to include in our routines, but we can still play to our strengths. Level 6 through 10 are called optionals because we have the option to do what we want. I'm happy to leave compulsories behind. I had a hard time with compulsories. All of us had the exact same routines. For me, some of the required skills were really hard.

"You are totally ready," Savannah says, agreeing with Lucy.

"You'll get your back handspring," Trista adds, and Lucy gives her a little smile of confidence.

"I'm going to kind of miss compulsories," Lucy admits.

"You will not!" Trista shrieks.

Then the girls all start talking at once about compulsories versus optionals. Maybe I should go immediately to Level 6. The girls training in the Level 6 and 7 groups are more my age. I look around at the table. As much as I love these girls, they are two or three years younger than I am. I'm in seventh grade while Trista, Carmen, Alexis, and Marissa are in fifth grade. Lucy and Savannah are in fourth grade. They are like sisters to me and I enjoy being their leader, but I'm also ready to train with girls my age.

I think about my situation as I watch Lucy's younger sister, Rose, join us at the table. She squeezes into Lucy's chair making me giggle. I hate that we are going to be splitting up. From what I can tell Lucy, Savannah, and Alexis will be moving to Level 6 and Trista, Marissa, and Carmen will be staying in Level 5.

And what will I do? I really want to move to Level 6 but gymnastics isn't that easy. I may have scored out today, but I do not have all of the requirements to compete Level 6. I wonder if my coaches, James and Melony, will even give me the choice to move up? Trista asked me what I am going to do as if it's all up to me. It's not all up to me. My coaches have to agree that I'm ready. I look down the long table to where our coaches are eating with our parents. I wonder if my score today will mean that they'll invite me to move up. I could see it going either way.

After dinner we file out of the restaurant with a lot of good-byes and 'see you Tuesday!' But I know I may not see some of them at my next practice. We will split up from here. I go along with the jovial goodbyes, but a part of me is sad at the reality of our group never being the same again.

Once we are in the car my mom immediately turns back to me. "James invited you to train with the 6s and 7s next week," she divulges.

"He did? Just like that?" I ask, surprised.

"Well, he thought you could try their workouts until the new year and then decide what you want to do," she explains.

"So, I'm not officially moved up?" I ask.

"I don't know, pumpkin, I just know he said, 'have Paige come in on Monday to the six-seven practice and see how it goes' and I said that you would like that. Did I speak too soon? Is that not what you want?" she asks, confused.

"No, it's fine," I assure her. "I'm just not sure if I'm on the Level 6 team or if this is some sort of trial."

She is quiet in response so my dad pipes up. "He said he wanted you there to see how it goes. What is there to debate? You scored out today, right?"

"I did. But I don't have a layout on floor or bars," I explain.

"Well, duh," my younger brother, Jason, pipes up. "It's a test. And you better pass."

Leave it to my brother to get right to the heart of the matter. He's right. I'm invited to practice, but not officially on the team.

It's a test and I better pass.

The following Monday at school I can't focus. All I can think about is that I'm going to practice today with the Level 6s and 7s. Half of my teammates aren't going to be there. What will the girls in the optionals group think when they see that I can't do a layout on floor or a back handspring on beam? In the past I've always moved up with my teammates. I've been with the same girls since Level 3. I've been with the same coach for that matter. Will James be coaching the Level 6s and 7s? Or will it be Katie? I know Katie is in charge of the optionals teams, but does that mean she coaches all of them? The upper optionals are there almost every day. They must take a lot of Katie's time. How did I not think to ask who is coaching the lower optional teams?

It doesn't matter anyway, I realize as I tap my pencil faster on my desk. I would want to be in the optionals practice today no matter who was coaching. It would have been nice to know. I sigh and look at the clock. Ten more minutes until lunch time. This day is crawling by. I look back down at my paper. I'm supposed to write something about what we just read. What did we read? I flip over the paper on my desk and reread the story that I didn't retain the first time. It's a terrible story about ocean garbage and I dread writing something about it.

Finally, the bell rings and I shove my blank paper in my backpack and head out the door to find my friends. I've been going to this school since kindergarten, so the transition to middle school hasn't been as bad as it must be for other kids. We have a homeroom which is two hours and then we rotate to our other four classes. That was an adjustment, but other than that, it feels the same. Most of all, I have the same friends.

I find our table in the cafeteria and flop my backpack down to dig out my lunch. Abigail quickly joins me followed by Katherine.

"I hate having science before lunch; it makes me nauseated," Abigail declares.

"It wasn't that bad," Katherine comments.

"What did you do today?" I ask, pulling out my lunch and setting my backpack on the floor next to me.

"All our teacher can talk about is how we're going to dissect frogs. It's so gross," she answers.

"I don't know what you're going to do when we actually get to the part where we really do dissect it," Katherine comments.

"Be absent that day," Abigail says smartly.

"How was your weekend?" Katherine asks me. "Didn't you have a big meet or something?"

"Yes, we had our State Championships. We placed second," I answer with a smile.

"Out of how many?" Abigail asks.

"I don't know, a lot. At least ten teams."

"Did you win the all-around?" Katherine asks, not really understanding how hard that is to do in gymnastics.

"No, but I scored out," I share.

"What does that mean?" she asks.

"It means I can go to the next level. Today in fact," I add.

"You don't have tryouts or anything?" Abigail asks. Abigail and Katherine are both dancers and they are always trying out for one team or another. I don't really get it, probably how they don't get gymnastics.

"No tryouts. We just have to get a certain score in Level 5 and the new Level 6 skills before we can move up. Come to think of it we sort of do have tryouts. It's just usually called testing day or an intrasquad."

"So you're not doing that this time? You just move up today?" Katherine asks.

My stomach sinks as I think about her question," I don't know."

"Paige, how do you not know?" Abigail laughs.

"I'm invited today or this week, I think, on a trial basis. I'm pretty sure I have to get some skills to stay," I finally admit out loud.

"Sounds stressful," Abigail says.

I don't comment creating an awkward silence, which is rare for our threesome. "Wanna see the dance we made up this weekend?" Katherine asks.

I nod yes and she pulls out her phone. I watch the two of them on the little screen and their silliness makes me laugh. I feel lucky to have these two friends at school. It seems like I had so many friends when we were little and our group got smaller and smaller as we got older. I ended up staying friends with Abigail and Katherine because we live near each other and we all like to dance when we hang out together. Although, I haven't done much hanging out with them since I moved up to Level 5.

"Now that your competition season is over are you going to be able to hang out this weekend?" Abigail asks, looking up from the video.

"I don't know, maybe. I think I might be going right into another season," I admit.

New Challenges

"You don't seem to know much about your new Level. Find out today and let us know," Katherine orders.

She's right. I don't know much about my new level.

Chapter 2

I walk into the gym in my favorite red and gold leotard with my gold shorts and a sweatshirt zipped over the top. My curly red hair is pulled back in a low ponytail. I wear either a low pony or double buns because I do a back extension roll on beam. The high ponytail or single bun get in the way and hurts my head. I walk upstairs to our team cubbies and see Savannah there stuffing a sweatshirt into her cubby.

"Think we'll get to use the optionals room?" I ask her pulling off my sweatshirt and throwing it in my cubby. We *are* working out with optionals today.

"I'm not sure, so I figured I'd use this," she answers,

referring to our personal cubbies we earned back when we got our kip in Level 4. I nod in agreement and put my shoes in my cubby.

"Are you nervous?" she asks me.

"Yes. Are you?" I ask her.

"Yeah. And it was weird coming here without Trista," she admits.

"I bet." Trista and Savannah are neighbors and Trista has been on our team since Level 3. It will be odd not to have some of our teammates here. We are silent as we walk downstairs and into the training area for our new practice.

Katie, the Optionals Coach, sees us as soon as we push through the glass doors. "Paige and Savannah!" she exclaims, and we walk over to her. "Welcome to optionals! We'll start running in a few minutes when everyone is here. For now, let me introduce you to the team." She yells over to some girls who are on the trampoline and they trot over to us. "These are my only returning Level 6s, Riley and Victoria. This is Paige and Savannah." The girls politely say hi and quietly observe us.

"Oh look the rest of my new 6s," Katie exclaims. "Over here girls!" she yells. "Alexis and Lucy, this is Riley and Victoria," she repeats.

We all say hi again and then Katie tells us to run ten laps. As I'm running I notice my former coach, James, over on bars with the little Level 3s. I give him a wave as we run by and he waves back. It's weird that he's not coaching us. I'm a little nervous about being trained by Katie. I've seen her with the Level 8s, 9s, and 10s and sometimes she seems intense.

By the time we finish our ten laps the rest of the lower-level optional team has arrived. "Stretch lightly while I introduce everyone again. Then we'll do complex."

The girls flop into splits and start chattering amongst themselves. I turn to my old teammates Alexis, Lucy, and Savannah and they seem as unsure as I do. As the oldest, I used to be the leader of this group. But it seems weird to still act like their leader when I have no idea what to expect and I'm no longer the oldest. The 6s and 7s look like they are all in middle school like me. Alexis, Lucy, and Savannah seem young for this group.

"These are our 7s over here," Katies says to us, standing near four of the girls. I listen as I switch to my left splits. "This is Aubrey," she says walking over to a girl and pointing to her as she adjusts her splits, "Brooklyn, Payton, and Maya. Girls these are your new 6s; Savannah, Alexis, Lucy, and Paige." We say an awkward hi making Katie chuckle. She tells us we have five more minutes to stretch whatever we need to before complex. Then she walks away and into the coaches' office.

We quietly do as she says, stretching our legs, backs, wrists, and necks.

"What school do you guys go to?" Peyton asks.

Alexis answers first, "I go to Mountain View Charter," she answers.

"What grade?"

"Fifth," Alexis answers.

"Are you going to stay there for middle school?" Brooklyn asks, knowing that Mountain View goes all the way up to eighth grade.

"Yeah, all my brothers go there. Except my oldest brother," she adds.

New Challenges

"I go to Hilltop Elementary," Savannah supplies.

"What grade?"

"Fourth,"

"Wow! You guys are young," Brooklyn comments.

"I'm in seventh grade," I say, saving my teammates from feeling bad for being young. "I go to St. Mary's."

"That place is supposed to be hard. Is it?" Maya asks.

"I don't think it's that bad, but I don't know any better. I've been going there since I was little."

"And what about you?" Peyton asks Lucy.

She shyly says, "I don't live near here. I go to Reagan Elementary downtown. I'm in fourth grade, like Savannah."

"We're all in middle school. Snowcap Canyon Middle School and Mountain View. Your brothers might know Peyton and Maya," Brooklyn says to Alexis.

"Stand up for complex!" Katie yells as she walks back to us.

The girls stop talking and do as Katie says, standing up and forming three lines on the floor for complex. I'm nervous as I get in line. Last summer I trained with the Level 6 and 7s when my teammates were at different gymnastics camps. I wasn't expected to do everything in the complex. Today I feel like I should be able to do everything Katie calls out if I want to be a Level 6. Am I officially a Level 6? I don't even know. I was just invited to workout with them. Is this like an interview? If I can't cut it, do I go back to the Level 5s?

I look at my teammates who are also here at their first day of Level 6. They have instinctively lined up behind me.

"Let's do three lines of three. Lucy or Savannah, come

over here to Aubrey's line." I see Lucy and Savannah exchange looks and without a word Savannah slowly walks over to the back of a line of Level 7s. Lucy, Savannah, and Alexis are as nervous as I am. I don't know why. The three of them scored out weeks ago and even had time to start learning their floor routines over the last few weekends. Clearly, they are going to stay in this group.

"Handstand walks!" Katie yells. We are starting with handstand walks? Usually James starts us with handstand forward rolls. I take a deep breath, this is optionals. Level 6 and up is serious business I think as I kick up into a handstand and walk on my hands about ten feet before I step down.

"Count your falls; ten push-ups for each fall. Do them when you get to the other end of the floor," Katie instructs.

I quickly kick up and make it another ten feet before falling. By the time I get to the other end of the floor I have fallen three times, so I start my thirty push-ups. Thankfully other girls fell too and are doing push-ups. I notice Brooklyn and Peyton are standing talking while the rest of us are doing push-ups. Which must mean they made it across the entire floor. Impressive.

As girls finish their push-ups and start standing up Katie calls out front and back walkovers and my line begins without me. By the time I finish my push-ups Alexis, who was at the back of my line, is starting her turn. I jump up and get ready to take my turn doing walkovers.

My walkovers are terrible because I have bad shoulder flexibility. Katie knows this and doesn't say anything. I get through them as best as I can. As soon as I finish she says, "Power hurdle round-off back handspring!"

Usually we warm-up with just the power hurdle round-off and then on the next turn we do the round-off back handspring. Apparently, in this group, they skip that step. Thankfully, I can do round-off back handsprings with no problem and I breeze through that skill and so do my teammates. Then she yells, "Round-off back tuck!" Wait, what? *A round-off back tuck with no back handspring?*

I'm glad I'm now at the back of my line as I watch Lucy, who is at the front, pause and think about what Katie just said. Of course, Lucy takes her turn and does a perfect round-off back tuck. Then Alexis steps up after her and does a decent back tuck out of her round-off. I stand at the edge of the floor. It's my turn, but I can't move.

"You can do the round-off back handspring again if you want Paige," Katie yells over to me, obviously aware of my hesitation.

I look over at her and she smiles at me, making me brave for the moment. "Can you spot me?" I ask. She nods and walks over to my side of the floor.

"Have you ever done a tuck out of a round-off?" she asks me. I shake my head no. "You're going to love it. Remember, feet behind you on the round-off to set," she says, and motions for me to go. I take a deep breath, power hurdle, round-off, and set (as she reminded me) so that I go up instead of back. I reach up, lift my knees, feel her hands on my back and waist, see the ground, and land. "No problem," Katie says, as I land safely.

I look up in shock. "That *was* easier!" I exclaim.

"Good, because it's probably going to be your series on beam."

A round-off back tuck on beam? That sounds exciting

and scary at the same time. I quietly nod and get back in line to wait for the next skill. She has us do front handsprings, front handspring dive rolls, aerials, leaps, switch leaps, and front tucks. Then she calls out a few odd combinations 'just for fun' like hitch kick aerial and round-off straddle jumps. I liked trying the different dance and acro combinations.

By the time complex is over I am beat; and we are just beginning. Katie tells us to grip up and go to bars. We go upstairs to get our grips. Alexis, Savannah, Lucy, and I stop at our Kip Club Cubbies while we watch our new teammates continue to walk to the far side of the room and through a door that says 'Optionals.'

"Do you think we go in there?" Alexis asks.

"Our stuff is here," Lucy points out.

"Yeah, but we're Level 6s now," Alexis persists, "shouldn't we put our grips on in there?"

All three of them look at me. But I'm not sure what to do.

"I can ask Katie about it," I slowly say as I watch Savanah pulling on her pink wrist bands. "Let's just grip up here for now," I suggest, not at all sure if that's the right answer. Barging into the optionals room where we haven't been invited seems weird.

Just then Maya pokes her head out. "You guys can come in," she yells over to us, making several parents turn their heads. "Grab your stuff," she adds in a lower voice.

The girls look at me and I shrug, "We can put our grips on in there," I agree. We grab our grip bags and walk over to where Maya is holding the door open for us.

I have only been in this room once before. There is a

desk along the wall where we entered. Across from us there is a big window that looks down on the parking lot. Along the other two walls there are lockers and in the middle of the room there are chairs, a bean bag, and a table. The girls are standing by their lockers putting on their grips.

Four of the lockers are decorated with our names on them. One for me, Lucy, Alexis, and Savannah. They carefully cut our names out of construction paper and taped them each to an empty locker.

"Wow," Alexis says, and I see the girls smiling at us.

"This is so nice!" Savannah exclaims.

"But what if I don't end up competing Level 6?" I ask Maya.

"Oh, you're stuck with us now," she says unconcerned. "Even if you don't compete, you'll stay in our group and work Level 6 and 7 skills," she reasons with confidence.

What she says makes sense. I smile a small smile and walk toward my locker and open it up. It is empty and clean inside so I set my grip bag down in it. "Thanks you guys," I say to them as I pull out a wrist band.

"It was fun," Brooklyn admits, "I like projects like that."

"It was fast though. We had to have Katie let us in yesterday," Aubrey says.

"I'm glad you did," Lucy says, opening her locker.

"Okay, we better hurry, we've been up here longer than usual," Maya points out and we quickly finish putting our grips on and run back downstairs for our bars workout.

Chapter 3

Katie has us warm up on bars similar to how James does, with push away kips. It's weird to have someone besides James coaching us. I look across the gym and watch him with the Level 3 girls on floor. They are sharing the floor with two other classes of recreational kids.

"Paige, you're up," Katie says to me. I look back at the bar in front of me. I jump into my glide kip and do three push-away kips. I hit my feet on the third one. I try so hard not to, but it still happens.

"You're going to have to have abs of steel to keep those legs up," Katie comments, "I can help you with that." Great, I have a feeling that is going to equate to rough conditioning. "Other than that, pretty good." I'm in a support position after my third kip and I nod in acknowledgement.

When I jump down she says, "When you're done warming up go to the pit bar and work flyaways without the tap swings before it."

"Out of a cast?" I ask her.

"Yes, start in a support position and swing down and flyaway. If you need to do the flat backs at first, that's fine."

I nod and get back in line for another set of push away kips. I forgot that Level 6 doesn't have tap swings in front of the flyaway. How am I ever going to do that? It sounds scary. I look over at James again. I wish he was coaching us.

I finish my push away kips and head over the pit bar with my old Level 5 teammates. The original Level 6s and 7s are told to do three of each half of their bar routine. The first intrasquad is in a few weeks, just before Thanksgiving. They are already doing routines.

"We have some serious catching up to do, huh?" Lucy asks as we walk up to the pit bar.

"Looks like it," Alexis agrees.

"We don't have to compete this season," Savannah reminds us. "We can just train Level 6 all year and compete next January."

"Is that what you're doing?" Lucy asks her as Alexis climbs up to the pit bar and starts pumping a few swings.

"I don't know," Savannah admits. "James said it was an option for me, but I can tell my mom really wants me to compete this winter."

Alexis swings into a kip and looks down at Savannah from her support position on the bar. "What do *you* want Savannah?"

"No talking up on the bar!" we hear Katie yell over to us. Alexis quickly takes her turn by pushing out, swinging down, letting go of the bar, and falling to a flat back. She did the timer drill rather than the actual flyaway.

"Have you ever flipped it out of a cast?" I ask her.

"Yeah," she says as she climbs out of the pit. "I did a few with my mom at summer camp. It's been a while though."

I nod and watch Lucy climb up. She swings, does a kip, cast, and a perfect tuck flyaway into the pit.

"That was beautiful. I didn't know you could do those," Alexis comments, sitting on the edge of the pit.

"We learned them both ways at Salt Lake Gymnastics," Lucy says. Lucy came to our gym in the middle of the Level 5 competition season. I realize now that when she came here we were only working routines and I have no idea what optionals skills she may already have.

"Do you have all of your Level 6 skills?" I ask her.

"I think so. I'm not sure which ones are Level 6 versus 7, but I'm pretty sure I have everything I need for Level 6. Except the back handspring on beam," she reminds me.

Lucy had her back handspring on beam a few months ago. But when James saw that she was doing it with her wrong hand in front he made her change it. Changing a skill is difficult; worse than learning it the first time.

I watch as Savannah easily does a flat back drill out of a cast. Now it's my turn. I know I can at least do the drill. I climb up to the high bar over the pit and do a pull up, pull over to get up. Then I pause in a support position thinking about what I need to do. I need to push away, like in a baby giant, but then at the top of the swing let go for a flyaway. I take a deep breath, cast and push away from the bar. I swing down and as I come up it feels too scary and fast to let go, so I decide to hang on. I swing up and back doing high tap swings.

"Let go!" I hear Alexis say.

On the second swing I let go and fall to a flat back. Of course, letting go on a tap swing is what we have been doing all season.

Disappointed, I climb out of the pit and watch Alexis jump up. She climbs up to the high bar, tap swings, kips up and pauses like I did.

"You've got this Lexi," Savannah says to her.

Alexis pushes away, swings down, and lets go at the top of her tap swing. Even though she keeps a straight body, she rotates a little father than falling straight to her back. She gives a little squeal as she lands in the pit on her upper shoulders with her feet up like a candle stick.

"You could have flipped that one," Lucy comments.

Alexis says something, but she is muffled within the foam squares of the pit. We wait for her to wiggle into a sitting position. "That was scary. I don't want to flip just yet." She climbs over the foam squares making her way to the edge of the floor where we are standing.

"You'll get it fast I bet," Lucy insists as Savannah jumps up for her turn.

We do this three more times. Savannah doing perfect drills, Lucy doing beautiful flyaways, Alexis over and under rotating her flat back, and me not letting go at all. I sigh, I wish James was here. He would know how to help me.

"Go smaller Paige," Katie says to me as she walks up. I look at her, "What?"

"Go smaller on your cast so it doesn't feel out of control. After you get used to a flyaway out of a cast you can slowly try it out of a bigger cast," she explains.

I nod, acknowledging that I heard her and wait for my turn. She gives Alexis a similar correction about controlling her cast so her flatback is controlled. Then she compliments Savannah and tells her she can flip her flyaway when she is ready. I notice she doesn't offer to spot; she simply tells her she can do the skill when she's ready.

"Lucy, have you done these on the regular set?" Katie asks, referring to the set of bars that are not over the pit. Lucy nods. "Then what are you doing over here?" she asks.

"You said for all the new 6s to go to the pit, so I did," Lucy explains.

"Yes, but you trained a little differently at Salt Lake Gymnastics," Katie says. "I'm guessing you have some of your Level 6 and even 7 skills." Lucy quietly nods in agreement. "Next time speak up and I will keep you with the returning 6s or even the 7s, depending on what we're working on."

"Okay," Lucy agrees, but I can tell she's not sure about it. I can't say I blame her. She just got used to us and now she may have to train with a whole new group of girls.

"Who's up?" Katie asks.

"I am," I answer and quickly get up to the high bar using a pull up, pull over.

"Kip up next time," Katie instructs when I get to a support position. I nod, knowing that is going to be so much harder. "Now, just do a little cast. Control your swing into a nice and easy flat back."

I take a deep breath and cast small, push back, and swing into a fairly slow tap swing. She's right, I feel more in control. My feet barely make it up to horizontal and I let go and float down into the pit with a flat back.

"There you go, Paige," Katie says, sounding pleased.

Maybe Katie isn't so bad after all.

After bars we have an uneventful vault rotation. The four of us who are new are vaulting onto mats. We are doing Tsuk and Yurchenko drills. The other 6s and 7s are doing Tsuk and Yurchenko entries. They vault up onto the table and have a large stack of mats behind the table. The official Level 6 and 7 vaults are entries, or timers, for the bigger Level 8 vaults.

Katie informs me that with my shoulder flexibility, or lack of, I should be training Tsuks, which I already figured.

"Do you want me to keep doing the Yurchenko drills?" I ask her.

"Nope. That's the beauty of optionals. You get to spend your time developing your strengths. Stick with the Tsuk timers."

I nod and get back in line.

I look over at the table where the girls are vaulting and I wonder how fast we have to transfer from drills to timers. It's November and the first optionals meet is in January. I feel like we are expected to make this transition fast and right now it's feeling overwhelming.

When we are done with vault Katie tells us to rotate to

floor. I get a drink of water and head to floor where James is waiting for us. I walk up to him and ask, "You're coaching floor?"

"Yep. Katie is with the upper optionals and I'm done with the Level 3s. I coach the end of your workout."

I'm relieved. James knows where I am in the process of learning a layout and he is a good spotter.

The girls don't seem surprised to see James as they get to floor. It must be something he does every week. I never thought about what James was doing when we weren't training with him.

"Hi ladies. Katie said you already did complex, so let's start by doing tucks and front handsprings on the diagonal. And two dance throughs each."

"We don't have floor routines yet," I remind him.

"I have mine," Lucy pipes up.

"Okay, yeah, Lucy has hers she brought from Salt Lake Gymnastics. But we don't," I say gesturing my hand to Alexis and Savannah.

"Yeah, we do," Savannah pipes up.

I turn to look at her, "You do?" I ask.

"Yeah, we've been coming in on Saturdays and Sundays to learn them," she informs me.

Wow, I knew they started learning routines, but I didn't realize they had their routines.

"You both have one?" I ask. They nod with a bit of sympathy in their eyes. I turn back to James, "Correction, I don't have a floor routine," I tell him, feeling left out and a little foolish.

"Don't worry Paige, you're a great dancer. You'll learn your new routine quickly. It won't be a problem. For today, do five of your front tumbling pass and five of your back tumbling pass."

"What are my passes?" I ask, trying not to get frustrated. How does everyone else know what's going on and I don't? It was easier when we were all training the same skills. At least I knew what I needed to get.

"Your back tuck for now, and hmm, let's try some bounders with you. We should get rid of the front handsprings as soon as possible," he thinks out loud.

"What are bounders?" I ask, but he doesn't hear me. He has turned to Lucy, Savannah, and Alexis and is giving them instructions.

They all have the same passes. They are to work round-off back handspring layouts and front handspring dive rolls.

As they all walk to a corner to warm up James turns back to me, "Why are you frustrated Red?"

"Everyone else knows what they're working. When did those three get routines and I didn't?" I sulk.

"Paige, I didn't know if you would score out of Level 5. All three of them had to score out before Melony created a routine for them. You'll catch up," he says unconcerned. He sees my frown and continues. "This is what you have been waiting for! Optionals is going to be great for you. We can pick skills that you're good at. Your shoulders won't hold you back anymore!"

His speech helps me calm down a little. He's right, I've been hoping to make it this far for this very reason. To have options.

"Today, instead of working front handsprings I want you to try front tuck, front tuck."

That sounds hard. And fun.

"How?" I ask curious.

"Go get your steps and do a front tuck landing about two feet in front of the pit. When it feels good, do a second one into the pit. I also want you to try punch, punch, punch front onto an 8-incher. Put the 8-incher along the edge. You won't be using the diagonal for these."

"Okay," I say, and turn to go get an 8-incher. I pull one off the stack by the stereo and throw it on the edge of the floor. I do as James says and stand with my arms over my head and hop on two feet in a punch. When I get two or three good ones in front of the mat I try to flip a front tuck onto the mat. I land on my bum on the very edge and roll back onto the floor.

"What are you working?" Lucy asks.

"Punch, punch, punch-front," I answer getting up.

"We used to do those." Of course she did. "Try starting your punches at the edge of the mat and work backwards to get your steps."

I nod. It's good advice. I start with the mat at my heels and punch away from it to see how far I travel. Then I turn around and go back the other way and this time I land on my bum in the middle of the mat.

"That's it Paige, keep your arms up and bend at your chest, not waist!" James yells at me from the diagonal.

I nod to indicate that I heard him, get up, and try again. It is kind of fun to be working something that no one else on my team is working. Maybe I am going to like optionals after all.

I'm grateful James is coaching us, even if it's only for a few rotations a week. He always seems to know how to coach me.

Chapter 4

When I walk up to our table at lunch Abigail and Katherine are hunched over Katherine's phone. I take a seat across from them.

"What are you guys doing?" I ask.

"Trying to pick out a song for a dance we're going to make up today," Abigail answers.

"That sounds fun," I say digging in my backpack for my lunch.

"You can come, but we know you have practice," Katherine adds.

"Actually I don't," I say, pulling out my lunch and setting down my bag.

"You don't?" they both say.

"What happened?" Abigail asks.

"I don't have practice on Tuesdays anymore because I changed teams," I explain.

"So you are officially on Level 6?" Abigail questions.

"Yeah, and they workout on Monday, Wednesday, Thursday, and Saturday."

"You passed the tryouts!" Katherine squeals, "Why didn't you tell us?" she asks.

"Because I wasn't sure. But I think it will stick. I'm not going back to Level 5." James is right, optionals is a good place for me and I shouldn't go back to Level 5, even if I don't compete in January.

"Well, that's cool," Abigail says. "You have Fridays off now," she points out.

"And you can come over today! Oh please, you never hang out with us anymore," Katherine pleads.

She's right. I don't see these two as much as I did when I was younger. I always eat lunch with them but outside of school I have been spending most of my time with my gym friends. "I'll ask my mom when she comes to pick up Jason and me."

Satisfied they both go back to picking out music for their dance they plan to create this afternoon.

When school is out I find Jason and we stand on the edge of the curb waiting for our mom to pull up. When we see her I walk up to the passenger window, "Can I hang out at Katherine's today?" I ask.

"Oh, pumpkin, that would be great!" I frown, she's a little too excited. She thinks I spend too much time with my gymnastics friends and worries that they are not my age.

"You know the Level 7s are my age," I sass.

"I know Paige. It's just that school friends are important, too."

I open the door for Jason and tell him I'll see him in a couple of hours.

"I'll have Dad get you on his way home," my mom says. I nod and shut the door. Then I turn back to find Katherine waiting for her mom.

When her mom pulls up all three of us pile in the car and Katherine and Abigail immediately start chattering about who they got paired up with in science. My mom is right; it is good to have school friends who are my age. The thought makes me feel a bit like a traitor to my gym friends. They are good friends, even if they are younger.

When we get to Katherine's house her mom says she needs to finish up some work and tells us to help ourselves to a snack. Then she disappears with her laptop. Katherine opens the pantry while Abigail takes a seat at the kitchen counter. I follow her lead and take a seat next to her.

"Do you have Oreos?" Abigail asks.

"No we ate those yesterday," Katherine says, leaning into the pantry. She's standing on one leg with her foot against her ankle.

"Graham crackers?" Katherine offers.

"No," Abigail decides, clearly comfortable in Katherine's house.

"Oh, here are some Pop Tarts in the back!" Katherine exclaims and comes out of the panty with a box of Pop Tarts.

"Are you happy you got paired up with Quinn?" Katherine asks Abigail as she opens the foil packet.

"Yes and no," Abigail answers. "I'm glad I get to talk

to him every day, but it's a little stressful to do projects with him. I mean, what if I mess up?"

"You're supposed to do the projects together. There's nothing to mess up," I point out.

"I guess," she says. "But I want him to know I'm smart."

"Of course he knows your smart, you've known him since kindergarten," Katherine points out.

"It's different now," she says.

I'm not sure I understand how it's different. We have all known each other forever at St. Mary's. Of course Quinn knows Abigail is smart and is probably happy to be her partner because she is nice and funny, too.

Katherine puts the pastries in the toaster and taps her fingers on the counter while she waits.

"Who did you get paired with Paige?" Abigail asks me.

"Trey," I answer.

"Oh my gosh, Trey is so cute!" Abigail gushes.

"Yeah," I agree. "We've been friends since second grade. Doing the projects together will be easy."

"You should make him your boyfriend," Katherine says, handing us each a Pop Tart on a napkin and turning to put one in the toaster for herself.

"How do I do that?" I ask.

"I don't know, just ask him, I think," she answers.

"That would be weird. And it might make him feel weird and then our projects wouldn't be easy," I decide.

"Then Abigail you ask Quinn," she directs.

"No way, he can ask me," Abigail determines. "Besides, you go first. If you know how all this works, you get a boyfriend first and tell us how it goes down."

Katherine is quiet as she pulls out her snack from the toaster.

"I'm just not that interested in anyone at our school," she deflects and I start laughing.

"What! What's so funny!"

"Of course you are. You always have been. You're just as scared as we are on what to do about it," I call her out in a way my teammates would do. Straight forward and to the point.

She walks over to the family room just off the kitchen and plops into a stuffed chair. "It's just that I have cramps so bad I can't see straight much less think about what to say to a boy."

"Cramps from what?" I ask. They both turn and look at me like I'm crazy. "It's not like we've done any exercise today; not even in PE. We just learned about the rules of badminton."

"Are you serious, Paige?" Abigail says, recovering first.

Suddenly I feel embarrassed that I don't know what they're talking about. I'm not sure if I should pretend I know what's going on or come clean that I'm confused. I decide to stay quiet and see what they say.

"Paige," Katherine says, sitting up, "have you not gotten your period yet?"

Ohhh! That's what they're talking about. Duh, how did I miss that? "No, not yet."

"Might be a while, you're so thin. Isn't that, like, a thing for gymnasts?" Abigail asks.

"I don't know," I answer. I really don't know; all of

my teammates are younger than me. I guess my old teammates are younger than me. Some of my new Level 6 and 7 teammates are my age. I wonder if I'll ever be close enough friends with them to ask them when they got their period, or if they have gotten it yet.

"I think it's a thing," Abigail repeats. "I got mine the summer between 5th and 6th grade."

"Wow," I say. That's so young. I had no idea she was dealing with something so grown up.

"Don't worry Paige, you're not exactly that far behind. I just got mine six months ago," Katherine explains. "My mom says that's why the cramps are so bad. Because my body is still getting used to it."

"What does it feel like?" I ask.

"It's huuuurts," she moans rolling to her side in the chair and tucking her feet up.

"Like a stomachache?" I ask.

"No, like a dull ache all over my tummy and back. I don't know how to explain it," she says. "I'm so glad we didn't really do anything in PE. That would have been impossible."

"Why?" I ask.

"Because I just don't want to move. I want to sit right here and not move," she declares.

How the heck am I going to do gymnastics when I get my period if I'm not going to want to move? Hopefully Abigail is right and it's a gymnast thing to not get your period.

"It's not that bad for me," Abigail offers. "Everyone is different. For some reason I don't have hardly any cramps and my period is only a few days," she shares.

"Lucky," Katherine says.

Abigail regards her for a moment and then asks, "What are we going to do if all you're going to do is sit there?"

"We could paint our nails," Katherine suggests. "I have some new colors; one that's iridescent."

"I'll get them," Abigail says leaving the room to go get Katherine's stash of nail polish.

"What can I do?" I ask, seeing that Katherine is truly in pain.

"Why don't you get some paper towels so we can paint our nails right here and I don't have to move."

I nod and go to the kitchen and grab the entire roll and bring it back to the family room where Katherine is sitting. Abigail comes back with a shoebox full of nail polish.

We have a great time picking colors and painting each other's fingernails. I try the iridescent one. It turned out to be gray that shimmers purple when it's in a certain light. I can't wait to show it to my teammates. Katherine went with dark blue and Abigail did hot pink with sparkles over the top.

By the time my dad texts me that he is out front, Katherine and Abigail have moved on to their toes.

"My dad's here," I tell them and stand up and go over to my backpack.

"Oh, bummer. We'll get to your toes next time," Katherine announces.

"Sounds good," I say, slinging my backpack over my shoulder.

"Bye guys, feel better Katherine," I say.

"I will," she says, admiring her toes.

"See you tomorrow," Abigail says and I head out.

New Challenges

I climb into the car and my dad asks what we did.

"Painted our nails," I say holding out my gray iridescent fingernails.

"Wow, so trendy," he says surprised.

I admire my fingers, "They are, aren't they?"

Chapter 5

I'm having a great beam work out. All the other girls are working routines since they have an intrasquad soon. Even Lucy, Savannah, and Alexis have a beam routine. They are doing what Katie calls a routine A with a back walkover and when they stick five of those, they do three of routine B with the back handspring in it. Savannah and Alexis have their back handspring on high beam with a few mats stacked underneath. For now, Katie is letting them do their routines with the mats or on the medium beam.

My assignment is five back extensions rolls on high beam and round-offs on low beam. Today I feel ready to take my round-offs to a higher progression. I was so caught up preparing for Level 5 State Meet the last few weeks that I haven't had much time to focus on the round-off. I was doing them on low beam without really realizing that they are ready to go up to either the medium beam with mats or the high beam with mats. When the mats are stacked up they seem the same to me.

I ask Katie if I can try them on a high beam with mats. "Do them on the medium beam since the girls are running routines on the high beams," she answers.

"Okay, can I have mats?" I ask.

"I don't think you need to, but do whatever you need to do to feel comfortable," she replies and turns her attention back to the high beams.

"I can help you," Brooklyn offers.

"Thanks," I say, surprised at the offer.

"I need the medium beam too and mats would be good," she says.

"Are you already done with routines?" I ask her.

"No, but I will be done with my five A routines soon and I need the medium beam to warm up my new series," she explains.

"Is the series in your B routine?" I ask her as we walk over to the stack of 8-inchers over at floor.

"Yes, I really want to compete it this season," she adds.

"What is your current series and what is the new one?" I ask her.

"In my A routine I do a back walkover back handspring. My B routine has a back handspring series," she says.

"Seems like they are both hard but I bet once you get

one you'll get the other," I comment as we pull off a mat and start dragging it over.

"Sort of, the back handsprings are just faster, which can be scary if you're off at all," she shares. "I see you're working round-offs. I think you'll be the only one on the team doing those."

"Yeah, I can't do back handsprings," I admit. Rather than asking me why, like most people do, she just nods in understanding as we slide the mat under the medium beam.

"Do you want one more?" she asks me.

"I kind of do," I hesitantly admit.

"Good, me too!" she says, making me laugh. We walk back to the stack of mats and drag one more over. "You compete back extension rolls, right? They seem way harder than a round-off," she points out.

"Seems like it," I agree. "It was my only option in Level 5 since I couldn't do back walkovers. The round-off feels easier, but I think if I don't make it, the falls are going to be worse."

"Totally," she agrees as we straighten the second mat under the medium beam. With two mats under the beam there is about a foot of space under it, making a round-off on the medium beam doable. "Who's up first?" she asks me.

I hesitate for a moment. Brooklyn is quietly eyeing the beam. "I can go," I say, and slowly climb up. She nods and goes over to a low beam to warm up her series. I stand up on the beam, walk to one end, turn around, and take a breath. I raise my arms and all I can see is the space between the beam and the mat. The mats aren't high enough to completely keep me from crashing. It's not like I can step down to them. "Maybe I need one more," I mumble and drop my arms.

"You can do this Paige!" I hear Katie yell over to me from three beams away. I look over at her not convinced at all that I can do it. "Think about the hand placement and twisting right over the top of the beam."

I look back at the beam. No getting out of it now, my entire new team is watching to see what I'll do. I raise my arms again and decide to go. I think about my hands and popping to my feet. I land with one foot on and I fall to the side onto my feet on the mats below. My heart is pounding so loud in my ears. I did it!

"Who-hoo!" I hear Savannah yell.

"That was high!" Brooklyn adds.

"Way to go for it," Alexis says.

"Thanks," is all I say as I climb back up. I want to go again before I lose my nerve.

"I did my round-off on the medium beam!" I exclaim as I open the car door and get in. "Oh I forgot," I say, shutting the back door and deciding to sit up front. I'm finally big enough to sit up front with my mom.

"No fair!" I hear Jason yell as I get in the front.

My mom ignores him and says, "That's great pumpkin. Is that one of the skills you need by the end of the year?"

"No, but I think I can compete it if I get it. I'm not

clear on what things I'm working that are required for Level 6 skills versus what skills are nice to have. But Katie seems to know all of it. I'm sure she'll tell me as we get closer."

"Seems like we're pretty close," my mom muses as she turns out of the parking lot.

"And I almost did bounders today on floor!" I continue, not deterred by my mom's comment about the time crunch.

"What's a bounder?" she and Jason ask at the same time.

"A front tuck right into another front tuck," I answer.

"I was able to do them onto a mat today. I mean, I landed on my bum, but I did them."

"Do you think you'll be ready in six weeks?" my mom asks.

I turn my head and smile at her. "I really do! Optionals is so much easier for me. Well not easy, but not as impossible as compulsories felt sometimes. I can play to my strengths. I can avoid doing anything that requires shoulder flexibility. James said it would be better for me. He was right. He's always right."

"Well, good. Because Katie emailed me today and asked if you could stay after on Saturday or come in on Sunday to get a floor routine."

"Yes! You told her yes, right?"

"I told her I would talk to you. A week ago you didn't even know if they would have you on the team. I didn't know what to say," she admits.

"I know. But now I finally get what optionals is all about and I think I can do it. Can I get a routine mom?

Please?"

"You're sure this is what you want to do? It's a much bigger commitment. Increasing from nine hours a week to twelve is a lot," she reminds me.

"It's what I want," I confirm.

"Okay. I'll email Katie back and see what time Melony can meet with you."

"Thanks Mom. If you weren't driving I would hug you," I say, making her laugh.

When I walk into the training room on Thursday I see James is standing with Katie on the floor waiting for us.

"Are you coaching us today?" I ask him as I walk up.

"Yes indeed. There are no compulsory girls in the gym on Thursdays so I help Katie with optionals," he explains.

"You never get a day off?" I ask.

"I get mornings and Sundays off," he offers. "Except on meet days."

"Where are my girls?" Katie mumbles, referring to her upper optional girls I saw running upstairs as I was walking in. I assume they are taking their time getting grips on. I know the upper optional girls start before we do and end after we do. I wonder how long their workouts really are.

"How long are they here?" I ask her.

"The 8s are here four hours, the 9s and 10s for five," she answers.

"Wow, and I thought coming for three hours at a time was a lot. I get hungry after only three hours."

"Bring snacks and eat them when you put your grips on," Katie says absently before walking away. Presumably to go tell her girls that their break is over.

"Hi ladies," James says, greeting Maya and Victoria. "Why don't you start running. The others can catch up."

We run in silence as the rest of the team trickles in. The gym seems different without any compulsory kids here. There are more rec kids in their absence.

"Come stretch over here, so these classes can get started," James says to us. We follow him to a corner of the floor and start stretching. "We will stay on this half of the floor and start with pit tumbling and then come back to floor for routines at the end of practice." This statement gets a loud groan from the girls. "I don't know what to tell you. The entire floor won't be open for a while. It's good conditioning to see how you throw a set at the end of practice anyway." The girls are silent and I'm glad I don't have a routine yet.

He tells us each what pass we are working into the pit and which pass we are to work when we get out of the pit and tumble back the other way. Most of the girls anticipated what they are to work and give him a quick nod and line up.

"Half of you line up here and half at that end so it rotates smoothly," he instructs. Then he turns to me. "Layouts into the pit and punch, punch, punch fronts headed back. The mat is already there for those who need it."

"Okay," I agree and I get in line to tumble into the pit.

New Challenges

For my first turn I just do a round-off back handspring in front of the pit to get my steps. Then I do the punch front drills on the way back. They are hard for me and I land the punch front on my bum. On my second turn tumbling into the pit James tells me to do the back tuck. Since I had to compete a round-off back handspring back tuck in Level 5, it's not a problem to do it into the pit.

"That was a little lower than usual, wait for the set," James corrects me as I climb out of the pit. "Do you want to do a layout on the next one?" he asks me.

I'm a little hesitant to do a layout after only one warm-up, but I realize I have some serious catching up to do if I'm going to compete so I nod yes.

"I'll spot," he offers.

"A big spot?" I ask, as I climb out of the pit and stand next to him.

"I guess it has been a while since you've done these. Was it the summer?" he asks me and I nod. Once the Level 5 season started last September, we stopped working Level 6 skills and focused on Level 5 routines. "Okay, big spot it is. You'll be fine. Nice tight set and pull your toes instead of your knees," he instructs.

"Toes," I say.

"And stay hollow," he adds.

"Toes and hollow," I repeat, and walk over to take my turn on punch fronts.

"Aubrey, are you twisting this one?" he yells over to the next teammate in line.

I'm thinking about the layout when I do my punch fronts and, of course, land on my bum. I'm going to have to learn to focus on more than one skill at a time. This group works hard and moves fast.

I get back in line for my turn at the pit and I watch Lucy do a beautiful layout with a tiny quarter turn at the end. I watch James laughing and talking to her. My guess is he told her to try a half twist and she was a bit cautious on her first attempt. I can't say I blame her. Then I watch Victoria do a layout with a half twist and I can see what James was trying to get Lucy to do.

It's my turn and I repeat James' corrections in my head before I take my turn. Tight, set, toes, hollow. The same thing as the back flip, just a little straighter.

"Layout!" James yells to me and I nod.

I run, do a round-off back handspring, set, pull my toes and I try to stay hollow but I feel like I'm not flipping very fast. I can feel James' hand on my back lifting me up and helping me flip. I panic that I'm not going to make it around so I bend at my hips in a pike position, which then speeds up my rotation and I over rotate into the pit.

"The first half was right, why did you pull it into a pike?" James asks me.

I struggle to sit up in the foam squares. When I finally do I answer him, "It felt so slow."

"It was a little, but I had you."

"I don't remember it being so slow last summer," I admit.

"It probably wasn't. You've grown a lot, so it's going to flip slower unless you set better," he replies.

"What?" I ask, as I stand up out of the pit.

"You need to set better," he repeats.

"No, about the growing."

"Paige, you've grown at least two inches in the last

four months. Layouts are a straight body, so the taller you are, the slower it flips. It's just physics," he adds, unconcerned. "Are you twisting?" he yells to Aubrey who is waiting for me to get out of the way to take her turn.

It's just physics, I think as I step out of the way so Aubrey can take her turn. It doesn't feel like physics. It feels unfair, I think as I watch petite Aubrey do a perfect layout full.

Chapter 6

"Oh my gosh, I finally feel better," Katherine says, plunking down in a chair across from me at lunch. This time I know what she's talking about.

"It lasts that long?" I ask, surprised and curious.

"Like three days that are impossible, and finally today I no longer have cramps. I'm still having my period. I'll be done by Sunday," she says, pulling out her lunch.

"A week then," I summarize.

"About a week," she agrees.

"I'm so glad it's Friday," Abigail says walking up. "I hate when teachers give homework on Fridays," she complains as she sits.

"You should be used to it by now. This place always assigns weekend homework," Katherine comments.

"What are you guys up to this weekend?" I ask them.

"Making up a dance tonight for dance company tryouts. You should join us," Abigail exclaims.

"Yeah, Paige. You used to be so good at making up routines with us. Didn't you say you don't have practice on Friday's anymore?" Katherine points out.

"I don't have practice," I say slowly.

"Yay!" Abigail cheers.

"But I was planning to go to PNO," I add.

"Remind me what that is. I remember you told us, but I forget," Katherine says.

"It stands for Parents Night Out. The parents drop off the kids and the kids play on the equipment for the evening," I explain.

"Sounds kind of babyish. I mean, aren't you allowed to stay home alone now that you're in seventh grade?"

"Well, yeah, I can stay home alone. I don't go just so my parents can have a night out. I go because it's fun to play on the equipment and work skills I don't usually get to work."

"You've been there all week. Don't you want a night off? You could hang with us."

"Pu-leese. Your choreography is the best! We miss it!"

I have been at the gym three days this week, which I am used to. Tomorrow I have my first Saturday morning practice for a new fourth day. Maybe I should rest up for the morning.

"Maybe," I say. As I start to cave, I remember Trista, Marissa, and Carmen. I promised my former teammates I would see them at PNO.

"Don't look so glum. I promise we're fun," Abigail says, noticing my torn expression.

I look up and smile, "I know. You guys are great. I would be lost at school without you."

"You'd be eating by yourself, that's for sure," Katherine teases.

"No, she'd probably get Trey to come over here and eat with her."

"What?" I say, surprised she pulled that name out.

"He's your lab partner, right?"

"Oh, yeah. Yeah he is."

"I've seen how he looks at you."

"Ooh, we can text him tonight and see if he likes her."

"Let's stick to making up a dance," I suggest. Thankfully, this redirects their conversation away from Trey and back to their dance tryouts.

It probably would be good to have a break before tomorrow's practice. I wonder if Alexis, Savannah, and Lucy are going to PNO tonight or if they decided to rest too? If I skip PNO, how am I going to explain my decision to my gym friends?

"How's the new level going anyway?" Katherine asks me.

"Good. I have a new coach for part of the time, so that's weird," I admit.

"It's more hours?" Abigail asks as she pulls out a baggie of cookies.

"Yeah. I went from nine to twelve hours a week," I say proudly.

"So are you exhausted?"

"So far it feels the same because I've only gone three days this week. Tomorrow morning is my fourth day."

"So you can't sleep over?" Abigail asks.

"Probably not," I confirm.

"Man, I think you should ditch gymnastics and do dance with us. There's more time to hang out."

"Not if we were good like she is. We'd have that many hours if we made the dance teams we tried for last fall," Abigail points out.

"You guys are good," I laugh. "We'll create something amazing for you tonight and you'll make this team."

When I get home from school my mom has to immediately take Jason to soccer practice. Well, not that immediately because he takes forever to find his shin guards and indoor soccer shoes. Usually, I go with my mom to take him and then she drops me off at practice. I don't have Friday practice anymore so I decide to stay home.

Once they're finally gone and I hear the garage door close, I flop into an overstuffed chair. It's kind of nice not having practice on Friday. I sit down and realize my body is tired and sore from working new skills all week. The house is so quiet. I wonder what I should do. I don't want to do homework just yet; I have until Sunday night anyway. Maybe I'll read.

I hear my phone ping from inside the front pocket of my backpack. Thankfully my bag is leaning against my chair and I don't have to get up. I lean over, unzip the front pocket and pull my phone out. It's a text from Trista's mom, which probably means Trista since she doesn't have her own phone yet.

> Mrs. Thompson/Trista:
> Hi Paige, Trista here. We are not going to Open Gym after practice. We're going to grab dinner and head back to PNO. Can't wait to see you!

Oh man, I have to tell her I'm not going. I really am torn. On the one hand, I want to see Trista, Marissa, and Carmen. But on the other hand, I don't want to be worn out for tomorrow's practice and I want to hang out with Abigail and Katherine. What do I say? I start at the phone, wondering what to reply.

> Me:
> Not going tonight, maybe next week.

Then I stare at the phone. I can't imagine Trista will take no for an answer that quickly.

> Mrs. Thompson/Trista:
> What?! Why?
> Me:
> Tired, big week.

The minute I send that excuse I regret it. Trista will be

mad if she finds out I lied or am not telling the whole truth.

    Mrs. Thompson/Trista:
>I heard you need to pick out floor music choices. We can just sit and do that? Not wear you out? We have some ideas for you.

    Me:
>Sounds fun, but I told school friends I would hang out with them.

I stare at the phone and no reply comes back. I know I just hurt her feelings. I'm the one that told her nothing would be different and that we'd see each other at PNO. And here we are at the very first PNO since our team split up and I'm already blowing it off.

My phone continues to be blank, making me feel incredibly guilty. I want to make sure she's not mad at me so I send her one more text:

    Me:
>What floor music did you have in mind for me?

I hold my breath waiting for it to ping back. When it does I feel relieved.

    Mrs. Thompson/Trista:
>Ballet music. Fancy music.

Her answer makes me laugh out loud.

Me:
> You mean classical?

Mrs. Thompson/Trista:
> Yes. From a ballet. Wanted you to hear it tonight. I can have Savannah's mom email it to you.

Me:
> Okay. Thanks Trista.

Then I think to add.

Me:
> You're a good friend.

Mrs. Thompson/Trista:
> Yeah, yeah. Have fun tonight. See you Wednesday.

Wednesday is the only day we are in gym on the same day. I set my phone down and lean back in the chair. This stinks. Why can't we all move up together like in other sports? I notice Jason's team all moves up together with their grade level. I feel my eyes flutter shut and I realize I really am tired from this week. Then I hear my phone ping again. I pick it up and look at it. It looks like I got an email. I open up my emails and see it's from Debbie, Savannah's mom. That was fast. Trista is probably at Savannah's house right now.

    I open the email and see there are three music files. I open the first one and it is beautiful, classical, and fast. I don't know if I can move that fast. There's an annoying part in the middle where someone says 'sample' over the top of the song. I have to listen a few times to hear the music during the interruption. I click on the second one. This one sounds similar, but not as fast. It sounds like it's from the same song, but a different section. I click on the third one and it is a recognizable Nutcracker song. I giggle, Christmas music would be kind of fun. But I think I like the first two. I glance up and read Debbie's message:

> Paige,
> You are such a beautiful dancer we thought these songs would be perfect for you. I can tell your mom what website to buy them from if you like any. The first two are from Swan Lake and the last one is from the Nutcracker.
> Debbie

I had the Nutcracker one right. Swan Lake; I think I like those two the best. I listen to all three of them again. Maybe Abigail and Katherine can tell me what they think. Although, it just won't be the same as my gymnastics friends weighing in on which music they like for me. They know where the tumbling passes would be and what kind of dancer I am in gymnastics. I sigh, maybe I should go to PNO. I hate this.

My mom comes in from the garage, "Are you going to PNO tonight pumpkin, or do you need to rest?"

"I don't know," I moan.

"Maybe you should take a break from the gym tonight so you can have a good practice tomorrow," she reasons as she shrugs out of her coat. "Man, am I glad it's Friday."

"Am I supposed to bring music?" I ask her.

"Oh yeah, Katie emailed me a few days ago. Sorry

pumpkin, I've just been so busy. You know how it is this time of year." My mom is a graphic designer for a marketing company. Every year she says all her major holiday projects will be done by Halloween, but they never are. "She gave us some websites where we can listen to samples," my mom continues. "You're supposed to bring your three favorite and I guess you decide with Melony tomorrow. And did you know you are staying after practice tomorrow? To work on the routine?"

"That part I knew. I didn't know I had to bring music choices. Debbie knew though," I comment.

My mom laughs, "That woman knows everything."

"She even sent me some songs I might like."

"That was nice. She's probably been listening to music for Savannah for months," my mom says.

"Yeah, probably. They're pretty cool. Here, listen." I play one of the Swan Lake songs from my phone.

When the song is done my mom says, "Oh Paige, that is beautiful. It would fit you perfectly."

"It might," I agree, "But can you give me the website and I'll listen to some of the other choices at Abigail's tonight."

"Sure. You're going to Abigail's?" she asks.

"She and Katherine are hanging out and asked if I could come. Can I?" I think to ask a little late.

"Of course," she smiles, pleased I'm not ignoring my school friends like I did all summer and fall.

Chapter 7

I arrive at Abigail's house with my phone fully charged and the website bookmarked so we can listen to floor music. They are dancers; they can weigh in.

I knock on the door and hear "Come in!" I hesitantly open the door.

"Hello?" I yell as I poke my head in.

"Back here!" I hear Abigail yell. I walk all the way in, past the entry way and kitchen and into the living room beyond that. I find Abigail and Katherine standing in front of a phone that is set up on a stand and facing them at almost their height.

"Hey Paige! Maybe she could record us. Would that be

better than the stand?" Katherine asks Abigail.

"Not necessarily because people bounce and shake and get funny angles. Plus if we keep the stand she can join us."

"Join you for what?" I ask.

"We're doing a TikTok video," Abigail explains.

"With the dance you made up for tryouts?" I ask.

"No, we haven't even started that yet."

That surprises me as I sit down behind the camera. "Aren't tryouts on Wednesday?" Maybe I have the week wrong.

"Yeah, plenty of time," Katheryn says as she walks up to the phone. "Okay, ready?" she asks Abigail and she nods.

She touches the phone and music comes on. Katherine backs up to stand next to Abigail and they start dancing in place. Their upper body is moving, but their feet are planted. It is the oddest-looking stand-in-place dance. I can feel a giggle bubbling up and I cover my mouth so I don't interrupt their video. A few seconds later they stop.

"That's it?" I ask, surprised at the brevity.

"We could go longer but TikTok likes short videos," she explains.

They immediately crowd around the phone to see their recording. They talk through the parts they like and don't like and then decide to try again. I watch them record the dance three more times, and honestly, all three versions look the same to me. But on the last one they squeal with delight that they nailed it and they happily post the video.

"Let's pick another one so Paige can join us," Katherine says, scrolling through her phone.

"Actually, I was hoping you guys could help me."

"Sure, what is it?" Abigail asks.

"I have to pick floor music by tomorrow," I say excited. They both blink at me and I realize they have no idea what a big deal this is. I have waited years to get my own unique music. "It's a big deal. The first time I get to pick. Can you just listen to a few with me?"

They nod and sit down on the big fluffy couch with me. I find the website and look at the menu. "There are tons here. Where should we start? Show tunes, hip hop, jazz, classical, soundtracks."

"Hip hop," Katheryn says. I click on the hip hop button and a huge list of songs come up. I start reading them off and the girls recognize most of them and ask me to play several. I select one and hit play. The instrumental version of the song comes on and I start trying to visualize how it would look to a floor routine.

"Why does it sound so funny? Why isn't she singing?" Abigail asks.

"It has to be instrumental," I explain.

"Well, that stinks. Her voice is what makes that song rock. Try another one." I click on another song we all know. But with the lack of singing, she's right. The song is kind of flat.

"No, that sounds wrong, too." I click to another hip-hop song and it has the same problem. It sounds all wrong without the artist. "Maybe let's try another genre. One that is instrumental to begin with," I suggest.

I click on soundtracks and these make Abigail and Katherine much happier. But they spend each song trying to guess what movie it's from instead of telling me if it would make good floor music.

"But which one should I pick?" I ask them.

"They're all cool. I like the Spiderman one, but that might be just because I like the movie," Katheryn admits.

"Tom Holland is so hot."

"Right? Did you see that dance he did on YouTube?" Abigail says, picking up her phone and pulling up the video for Katheryn to see.

This is a disaster. They have no idea what they are listening for. Why did I think I could pick out floor music with non-gymnasts? I sigh. I must decide by tomorrow. I don't have time to do this with my teammates.

I think about the email Debbie sent me. My teammates have already been thinking about my floor music (and theirs) for months. I bet they were listening to music for Savannah when they found songs that might work for me. I can envision Savannah and Trista listening to music endlessly.

"Hey guys, will you listen to one more?"

"Sure hold on." They are still huddled around a phone watching a video. When the video is done they look up expectantly at me.

"Okay, what do you think of this one for me?"

I press play on one of the Swam Lake songs. The girls are quiet as they listen. They are much more captivated than they were with all the other songs. When it is over Katheryn says, "Tchaikovsky's Swan Lake. Pas de deux. A beautiful piece Paige; I think you would rock it," she says in all sincerity.

"How did you know the song?" I ask, pleased she likes it.

"Duh, we have taken ballet for like, ever. And Swan

Lake is my favorite ballet of all time. Even though it's kind of weird. I love the music and when all the dancers become swans."

Of course, I should have known they would know a ballet. "You really think I could pull it off?" I ask, playing it again.

They are quiet as they listen again and finally Abigail says, "Totally. That one is perfect for you." I smile to myself. Trista and Savannah knew all along.

We spend the rest of the night scrolling through TikTok, picking out a video to copy, learning the choreography, and recording it. I don't really understand the point but it was silly and fun and made my friends happy.

I am still worried for them that they have to create something by Wednesday but they don't seem concerned about it, so I stopped bringing it up. I'm so used to planning ahead with gymnastics and being the leader with my team that I have to try to step back and just hang out when I'm with Abigail and Katherine.

By the time my mom texts me that she is on her way to get me they are talking about boys and who they should text.

"You know their numbers?" I ask, surprised.

"They're in the school directory," Abigail teases.

"Really?" I ask.

"No, Paige, don't use that! You'll get their parents. We have some numbers from the yearbook signings last year and from asking," Katherine explains.

"Asking? You ask boys for their number?" I ask flabbergasted. I would never have the guts to do that.

"It's helps when your lab partners and you can make up a reason to need his number," Katherine says, teasing Abigail.

"It worked," Abigail a says with a smirk.

I don't know what to say and thankfully my phone pings.

"My mom is here," I say standing up.

"Do you have to go so early? We're just getting to the fun stuff."

"I have practice in the morning," I say, half bummed and half relieved to leave before they start texting boys.

Chapter 8

The next morning I walk into Perfect Balance excited about practice. I'm pumped to stay after and work on my floor routine. We run our laps and are stretching when Katie comes up to us with a clip board.

"Who is staying after for floor dance?" she asks. Savannah, Alexis, Lucy, and I all raise our hands. "My newbies, good. All of you need it," she says unapologetically. We know we do. The other girls got their routines in August, when we were starting our Level 5 season. "Anyone else?" she asks looking up. "Madame Julia will be here and the new 6s aren't ready for her. So any of you who can stay and work on the fine details with

Julia should do so." Madame Julia is our ballet teacher. She is very picky when it comes to dance execution.

"I can stay," Maya says. A few of the other girls murmur that they will text their parents and see if they can stay.

"I told you guys last week," Katie says, frustrated.

They remind me a little of Katherine and Abigail procrastinating on making up their dance routine when I was there to help them and give new ideas. Now my new teammates have a chance to get help with Madame Julia and they are dragging their feet. I wonder if it's a teenage thing.

"The more you prepare now, the better you will score in January," Katie reminds them and they say nothing. "Keep stretching until James gets here. He'll decide where you start," she instructs. Then she leaves to coach the upper optional girls who have been vaulting.

"James is coming?" I ask.

At the same time Savannah asks, "How early do they get here?"

"Yes, James coaches us on Saturdays," Aubrey answers, "There are no compulsories on Saturdays. And Katie coaches the upper optionals the entire time."

"Unless he's at a meet," Peyton points out.

"Yeah," Aubrey agrees, "but meet season for compulsories is over."

"They get here an hour before us and stay an hour after," Brooklyn answers Savanah as Peyton and Aubrey keep talking about James' schedule.

"Wow," Savanah says under her breath. I can tell this rattles Savannah a little, but instead of saying anything she turns to me and asks, "Did you like any of the songs we picked out?"

"I think I like one of the Swan Lake ones," I share.

"I knew it!" she grins. "That one is perfect for you!"

"Can we hear it! Play it on the gym stereo," Brooklyn encourages.

"It's on my phone," I say.

"You can grab it when we go up to put grips on," she points out and I nod.

"Good morning ladies," James says walking up with a cap pulled down low over his eyes and coffee in hand. "What event do you want to do first?"

The girls call out four different events and James decides we are starting on beam. I think he already knew that because it doesn't look like he even heard us. I don't care how groggy he is, I'm just happy he's here to coach us this morning. Saturday morning may be my favorite workout of the week.

Saturday morning workout was the worst. Frist of all, we started on beam and my feet were still cold and every round-off stung. James let us stay in sweatpants or leggings, but, of course, we have to have bare feet for beam. Then we went to bars and the cold stung my hands and I got two rips. I haven't had a rip in a long time. James said it was from the increase in hours this week. Apparently my hands aren't used to it. Vault went okay because by then the gym was a little warmer, or I was, I'm not sure which. I never thought about how when we come in after school it is the warmest part of the day in Snowcap Canyon. Mornings here are cold. I'm going to have to wear long sleeves next week.

By the time we get to floor I finally feel warm. Most of the morning recreational classes are over by now and we have the entire floor to ourselves. The upper optionals have been waiting for the floor to be empty, too. I see them come over to floor as we are walking over. Uh-oh James and Katie didn't coordinate and now there are too many of us on one event.

"Five lines!" I hear James yell and that is when I realize we are all going to do floor together. With this many kids? I am supposed to do what a Level 10 is doing?

Wildly intimidated I get in line behind Peyton and I notice that my former Level 5 teammates all get in line behind me.

"Complex ladies. If you cannot do what I call out, do a modified version."

"Round-off back tuck! For my littles, do either a round-off or a round-off back handspring. The modification is your choice!"

Girls start doing sky high round-off back tucks. *Littles?* We are the littles now. With no Level 1-5 girls present, we are the littles. I look back at Savannah, Lucy, and Alexis and they are tiny compared the rest of the girls lined up. Peyton has taken her turn and I am up. I decide to do just the round-off and, of course, nobody cares. I turn and do a second round-off because I have room. When I get to the end of the floor, I get back in line behind Peyton. I look around at this big group of high-level gymnasts and I have to say, I like being one of the little ones for once.

"Front handspring!" James yells out.

We continue like this for another twenty minutes. Some of the skills James yells out are impossible, but there's always a smaller version we can do. And some of the combinations he calls out are fun to try. When we're done, I'm curious how this many girls are going to train floor. James announces we are tumbling on the diagonal and along two sides for tumbling drills. In addition we are to rotate to the red tumble strip and then over to trampoline. I notice no one is tumbling into the pit today.

"No routines either?" Brooklyn asks.

"Let's take a break from them. Maybe dance throughs at the end for conditioning," he muses.

I know by now to work punch fronts along the side where there is an 8-inch mat set out for us. For my turn on the diagonal I work layouts. Both Katie and James are spotting kids on the diagonal tumbling and I love the different passes the girls are doing. It's hard to work out when you just want to stop and watch.

I rotate to a diagonal corner and take a deep breath. Should I warm-up with a tuck or go straight to the layout? Thankfully James is standing at the other and of the diagonal and he holds up a fist, indicating a tuck. I nod and run and do a round-off back handspring back tuck. It's okay, but it felt sluggish. James must have not noticed because he just nodded and said, "Layout the next one. Let me know if you need a spot."

"I need a spot," I say quickly, making him laugh.

"Okay, do your bounders on the tumble track, front halves on the trampoline, and then come back over here for your layout," he instructs. The multiple stations keep us moving and I'm tired by the time I get back to the diagonal. I wait to catch James' eye and he holds up a straight hand indicating I am to do a straight body back flip, a layout. I nod, take a deep breath, and go. I do a round-off back handspring, and my take-off feels funny. I know better than to stop. I have to keep going and do the best I can. I pull my toes and try to stay hollow. I feel like I'm in slow motion and I'm not going to make it around. Thankfully, I feel James bumping my back, helping me get some height. I still feel low so I bend in the hips and change to a pike position rather than a layout. This change helps me flip faster and get to my feet. I land on my feet with my weight back on my heels. I fall on my bum as James stumbles past me after he sets me down.

"Why'd you pike halfway through?" he asks, coming back to where I'm picking myself up off the floor.

"It felt slow," I say, standing up.

"It was slow, but I had you,"

I nod, feeling silly I piked it. "Why's it so slow?" I ask him.

"Your back handspring is not the best technically so you're going to have to have a great set and nice hollow body to make it around," he says.

"But I've always had a bad back handsprings. This felt different," I try to explain.

James shrugs, "You're growing Paige. You're going to have to work through the changes and learn this skill despite the challenges," he says. His words seem unsympathetic, but his face is looking at me with pity. I have never seen that look before.

"But I've grown before and I never felt this . . . slow," I say.

"Well," he hesitates, "this time your center of gravity is changing."

Then he motions for the next girl to go and I step out of the way. I know I'm supposed to go over and work my punch fronts along the edge. I don't move. I need to know what he's talking about.

Lucy takes her turn doing a perfect layout and I wait for James to turn back to me.

"What's my center of gravity?"

He waves for Savannah to go and says, "Hang on." Savannah does a nice high layout and I'm not sure why James is even standing there for her. He gives her a quick correction and turns back to me.

"So Paige, when boys and girls are children all of them have their center of gravity between their shoulders, right here," he says, pounding a fist against himself just above his chest. "When girls go through puberty their center of gravity moves lower, to about their hips. This can be good on beam, because your balance is closer to the beam. It is not great for floor. You will have to get more height in your set to get your hips high enough for a flip. It's biology and physics."

"Biology and physics," I repeat, surprised by this new information about my body. Does it really change that much?

"It's also gradual, so you should still be able to do your skills." When I don't say anything he asks, "It has been gradual, right? Not a drastic change?"

"No, not drastic," I agree.

"You are strong Paige. You just have to use those legs and be more technically correct with your set."

"Okay," I agree. "I'll set."

I'm a little overwhelmed by this information but his answer satisfies me enough to walk away and over to my front tumbling. Now I'm behind Savanah and I watch her do a front handspring into a dive roll onto the mat. Then I do my front tuck into a dive roll onto the mat. She waits for me and we walk over to the tumble track together.

I am deep in thought over this center of gravity thing and Savannah doesn't seem to mind the silence. She starts her tumbling pass on the tumble strip. I take my turn doing front tucks. Then we make our way over to the trampoline. I have a great time here attempting front twisting. Soon enough I forget about my problems on the layout until it is time to rotate back to the diagonal.

I wait for James' signal. He is telling me to do a layout again. I take a deep breath and go. This time I think about my set, pulling my toes, and staying hollow rather than bending in the hips. I can feel James bump and catch me.

He nods when he sets me down. "Better."

"Still slow," I complain.

"I know. You're just going to have to work through it."

Through what? Feeling sluggish?

I don't say anything and go over to my front pass. My front pass is feeling weird too, although not as odd as the layout. Maybe back tumbling just isn't my thing.

The rest of floor is the same. I don't have a bad work out; I just feel like I'm not improving. Maybe I'm just tired because this is my fourth workout this week and I'm used to only three. Either way, I'm glad when James announces it's time for conditioning. As we start conditioning Melony comes over and pulls me, Savannah, Alexis, and Lucy from the group to work on our routines.

She turns to my teammates and says, "Do five of each leap pass to warm up and then do five of each dance section. We will run dance throughs after I am done here with Paige." They nod and get to work.

"Do you have music choices?" she asks me.

"I have three, but I'm hoping you like my favorite one," I share.

"Let's hear it," she says. I pull up the email, click on the song, and hand my phone to her. The Swan Lake song comes out tinny on my phone but I see Melony break into a big grin.

"This is perfect for you," she says as she turns up the volume. "Madame Julia is going to love it," she adds.

"I like it better than the others," I repeat. She hands the phone back to me.

"I'd still like to listen to your other choices," she says, handing the phone back to me.

I pull up another song and hand her my phone. It's the other Swan Lake song. "This is similar, what's the third one?"

I reach over and click on the Nutcracker song. "Oh, I love this!" she exclaims. I stand there nervous that she's going to make me use the Nutcracker song when I like the Swan Lake one. She is intently listening to the song and I am holding my breath to see what she says. "Beautiful choices. I could create something for you from any of them.

You pick," she says handing back the phone.

"Really?" I say relieved.

"Of course, you're the one that's going to have to listen to it a thousand and one times."

"Pas de deux then. The first Swan Lake one," I confirm.

"Perfect timing!" Melony exclaims as Madame Julia walks up. "Listen to Paige's music," she says, playing Swan Lake again.

Madame Julia listens quietly and then says, "Perfect for Paige, the dancer *and* gymnast."

"I agree," Melony says. Then she instructs Madame Julia on who she will be working with. "Maya is here to work with you and I think Brooklyn has stayed, too. They both need work on making everything in their dance bigger."

Madame Julia nods and goes over to where Maya has been working turns.

Melony looks at me, "Let's pick out your leap pass," she says.

Melony has me try several different leap combinations to see what I'm best at.

"When your split leap gets to 180 degrees it will be so pretty with your toe point," she comments.

We finally decide on split leap, split jump. Then she leaves me to work one and a half turns in front of the mirror while she helps my teammates with their dance. Turns are much easier for me than the leaps. I do turns until I have rug burns on the ball of my foot.

"Melony, do you want me to work something else?" I ask over to where she is helping Savannah with a dance sequence she doesn't seem to be getting.

Melony looks over to me and says, "You can be done for today. I will have some of your routine ready for you on Monday." I nod and walk over to Alexis.

"Are you about done?" I ask her.

"I think so. Either way, my mom is going to be here soon because we have to drive to a basketball game that is a few hours away." Alexis has four brothers. All of them except Drew play basketball and baseball. Drew is a gymnast like us. I search the gym and see Drew on the trampoline. He must have been here all morning. First with the boys' team and now just hanging out waiting for Alexis.

"Okay you four," Melony says walking over to us. "You can be done for today. Work on the dance at home. Paige, work on your splits." Then she looks around at the empty gym and adds, "Stretch while you wait for your parents."

We talk a little in our splits as we wait for our parents. My teammates are excited about my music and for me to get a routine.

"Trista is going to be excited when I tell her you picked one of the ones we picked out," Savannah says.

"You guys listened to a lot didn't you?" I guess.

"Tons. And whenever we heard the classical stuff we thought of you."

"Thanks, I really like it. I didn't think I was going to score out of Level 5 so I wasn't listening to music at all."

"They've got your back," Alexis pipes in. "Debbie has been listening to music since Savannah was a Level 3," she teases.

Savannah laughs good naturedly and then says, "Turns out it was a good thing."

"Yeah, totally," I agree.

When I get home from practice I flop into a chair in the family room. I am so tired. Beyond tired.

"Do you want some lunch?" my mom calls from the kitchen.

"Not really."

She walks into where I'm sitting and looks at me for a moment. "You look beat."

"I feel beat," I agree.

"Level 6 is hard, huh?" she comments.

"Yeah. But it's more fun. I get to work different skills."

"Why don't you go lay down and rest. You can eat after a little nap," she suggests.

I would like to just sit right here. Unfortunately, my brother bounces in with a stack of cards and asks if he can do a magic trick.

"I think Paige is going to rest," my mom says saving me. "Why don't you perform the trick for me?"

He runs over to her and tells her to pick a card. I drag myself out of the chair and up to my room before Jason sees I'm gone. Now that my mom mentioned it, a nap sounds like a good idea. I don't know why I'm so tired.

Today's workout wasn't that much harder. I didn't even do conditioning. Usually I workout three days and go to PNO. This week I did three days plus Saturday morning. It's not that different, so why do I feel so drained? I walk to my room and fall onto my bed. I don't even bother changing out of my leotard and sweats. I roll to my side, pull my blanket over myself, and drift off instantly.

When I wake I don't know what day it is. I look out my window and see afternoon light streaming in. Oh yeah, it's Saturday afternoon. I sit up, or evening? How long was I asleep? I reach over and turn my nightstand clock toward me. Four o'clock. Wow, I slept for several hours. My head hurts from being in a ponytail all day. I reach up and tug the rubber band out. My red curly hair sprays every which way. I run my hand through my hair, making it feel better but probably making my hair crazier.

I hear my stomach rumbling and realize I'm starving. I wander down the hall and find my mom doing laundry.

"Well hello sleepy head. Do you feel better?" she asks.
I nod. "I'm hungry."
"I'm sure you are. We had turkey sandwiches for lunch. I made you one and put it in the fridge," she says, reaching into the washer and moving clothes to the dryer.

"'kay," I say and shuffle off to find the sandwich. I make my way down to the kitchen. The house is quiet which means Jason is probably playing video games. I yank open the refrigerator door and find a plate with a sandwich sitting under plastic wrap. I pull it out along with some orange juice. Then I search the pantry and find a mini bag of chips.

I sit at the counter and slowly eat my lunch. My mom

comes down a minute later and pours herself a glass of juice.

"I got an email from Melony saying I needed to go online and buy your music," my mom comments.

"Yeah, we picked my music today."

"That's exciting, can I hear it?" she asks.

"It's on my phone," I look around. I don't even know where I dropped my gym bag. I still feel a little disoriented. "Why am I so tired?" I ask my mom.

"This was a big new week," my mom answers.

"Not really, my practices were still three hours each. I feel spent." I try to explain.

"I think you're growing." She comments.

"Why does everyone keep saying that?" I ask in frustration.

"Nothing to get frustrated about; you're twelve. This is when kids have growth spurts," she comments, unconcerned.

"I don't want a growth spurt," I pout, making my mom laugh.

"Of course you do. You don't you want to be 4'10" your whole life," she points out.

"Maybe I do," I grumble. "At least a little while longer anyway," I qualify.

"Let me hear your music again," my mom says, smartly changing the subject.

"You already heard it and I don't know where my gym bag is," I huff.

"I'd like to hear it again. You bag is by the door where you dropped it," she comments as she takes a sip of her juice.

"I don't feel like getting it," I snap at her. Why am I being so rude?

My mom looks at me over her cup. She nods and walks out of the room. Now I feel like a jerk. The worst part is that I want to share my music with my mom. I think she'll like it. Now what do I do?

I get down from the counter and go over to the front door to where my gym bag is flopped on the ground; just where my mom said it was. I rummage through and find my phone. I wander around the house until I find my mom folding laundry in her room.

"Mom," I say and she turns to me but doesn't say anything. I tentatively walk in farther. "I'd like you to hear my music," I say.

"I'd like that too" she says, pairing socks together.

"Sorry I was a jerk," I add.

She looks at me, holds my gaze and says, "Thank you."

It's an awkward silence for a moment and then she adds, "Paige, I know you're going through a lot with the new level, growing so fast, and trying to juggle school. But no matter how hectic things get, you still need to respect your mom."

"I know," I say, and I do. I honestly don't know what came over me.

She nods satisfied and picks up another pair of socks and says, "Let's hear it." I smile and scroll through my phone to Debbie's email. I find the right Swan Lake song and play it.

"I think that will fit you really well," she comments.

"I do too," I agree. "I bet Madame Julia will even help

me put in a few real ballet moves," I speculate.

"We have to buy it?" she asks. "To get a version that doesn't say 'sample' right in the middle?"

"Yeah, Savannah's mom sent the link and everything. After we buy it, we have to email the download to Melony and she will put it on the gym phone," I explain.

"And you're sure this is the one you want?" she asks me. "You listened to other choices?"

I smile, "I did. And I'm sure."

Chapter 9

It's the week of Thanksgiving so I only have school Monday and Tuesday and practice Monday and Wednesday. I'm hoping I can work on my floor routine this weekend. Melony got the music from my mom and said she would start creating something right away. She is aiming to have a routine for me by the holiday weekend. We usually go to my Aunt Jennifer's farm for the Thanksgiving weekend. Maybe Melony will finish it and I will have time to learn it before we go out of town. Sometimes my birthday falls on the Thanksgiving weekend. I haven't looked at a calendar, I wonder if it does this year.

"Why the frown?" Katherine says to me as she plops

down at the cafeteria table across from me.

"I was just wondering about our Thanksgiving plans this weekend," I share.

"We're skiing," she says. "We're staying in Park City for the entire weekend. My favorite part is the hot tub on the back deck."

"You're getting a hot tub?" Abigail asks, having caught only the last part of Katherine's sentence.

"No, we're going to a cabin in Park City with a hot tub," she clarifies.

"Lucky. I'm going to my grandma's house in Oregon," Abigail shares.

"That sounds fun," I say, wondering why she sounds bummed.

"It can be. But it can also be boring. She doesn't allow electronics so we have to, like, do puzzles and play board games the entire time," she complains.

"Not even movies?" Katherine asks in horror.

"Yes, movies, but only in the evening and everyone has to decide together so no guarantee the group picks a good one."

"Geez that's strict," Katherine says.

"Four whole days. At least my cousins can be cool," she admits.

"What about you, Paige? Are you going to the farm?"

"I'm not sure this year," I say slowly.

"What's not to be sure about?" Abigail asks me, taking a bite of her sandwich.

"I think I need to stay and work on my floor routine. Or rather, learn my floor routine," I explain.

"You can't take one weekend off?" Katherine asks.

"It doesn't seem like a good idea. I'm so far behind. All the other girls, including the other new Level 6s, have their floor routine. We have a mock intrasquad this Wednesday that I can't even participate in. By Christmas I'm supposed to be ready at a real intrasquad."

"That's a month away," Abigail points out.

"Is it a lot to learn in a month?" Katherine asks, trying to understand.

I nod, "It feels like it," I say.

"What do you have to get? Don't give me that look. Abigail and I did gymnastics before we decided to focus on dance. We aren't totally out of it," she reprimands me.

"Okay, I have to get my floor tumbling passes, my dismount on bars, and . . . and I guess that's it," I realize as I think about it. My vault is a Tsuk timer, which is really just a half-on. On bars I need to learn the flyaway from a cast, on beam I can keep doing my back extension roll, and on floor I need a layout. I'm not sure if I'm doing the bounder this season or not. I should talk to James or Katie. Or whoever is making my routines because I should know this.

"That's not that bad; you could take a Thanksgiving vacation to your aunt's farm," Abigail decides.

Maybe I could. Then again, everything in gymnastics is harder than it seems. At least for me.

The rest of the school day drags along. Teachers are frantically wrapping up units before we go on break. I keep thinking about the skills I need and how maybe I'm closer than I realized. I think I'm feeling behind because I don't have routines yet. Whenever beam or floor routines are assigned, I'm given a separate assignment. That brings me to the very reason I should stay, to learn my floor routine. I wonder if I can stay; I haven't even asked my parents. Would my entire family miss Thanksgiving so I can learn a floor routine?

When school gets out I find Jason at our usual spot. We stand by the curb to wait for our mom along with tons of other kids. It seems chaotic but the pick-up line is fairly organized. Cars roll up in the inside lane, pick up kids, and move to the outside lane. The cars have the last name of the children in their visor and as the car rounds the corner a teacher announces the name in a microphone and those kids run up to the front of the curb to be picked up. Our mom is later than usual to pick us up and I see her car round the corner before our name is announced.

"Green!" we hear as I take Jason's hand and walk to the curb. My mom pulls up and we quickly climb in. We know to chat after we're seated and buckled since she has to pull away from the curb quickly to let other parents in.

Since we're a private school, there are no buses. Every single kid has to be picked up in a car. Unless they walk, but very few kids live nearby. Most of my classmates are scattered all over the Salt Lake Valley. I'm lucky Abigail and Katherine live close to me. I think that's why we became friends. Our parents were able to get us together outside of school because we live near each other.

When we're finally leaving the parking lot my mom says, "How was your day?" I stay silent knowing Jason will answer.

"We got a classroom lizard!" Jason exclaims. "No one can decide on a name. I think it should be Lizzie."

"Your poor teachers," my mom says.

"Nuh-uh, they love it. Lizzie already likes my teacher the best. We vote on a name Tuesday. Is tomorrow Tuesday?" he asks.

"Yes. Tomorrow is Tuesday. You have school and then we're on break," she adds.

"Then I think we get a party tomorrow too," he says.

"Yes you do. Remember, you're having a Thanksgiving dinner at lunch. I have to send you with cranberries," she reminds him. Then she turns to me. "Are you doing anything in homeroom for Thanksgiving?"

"No, they don't do anything fun in seventh grade," I sulk.

"Oh, pumpkin, it's hard to grow up," she teases.

"When are we leaving for the farm?" I ask.

"After work on Wednesday. You're going to have to watch Jason on Wednesday while we're at work."

"When do we get back?"

"Probably Sunday afternoon so I have time to do laundry and settle in before another week of work begins."

"What about practice?" I ask.

"You can miss practice or we can leave right after practice."

"But when am I going to get my floor routine?" I ask, starting to panic. I know I was just thinking everything was going to be fine, but now I'm frustrated no one asked me about this trip.

"When we get back. The gym is closed anyway," she says.

"Not for optionals. It's never closed for optionals."

She turns and looks at me, surprised. "Do you have practice?"

"Well, no. I don't know. I mean, I thought Melony said she was going to have my routine ready."

"And it will still be here when we get back. Paige, it's four days. What's the big deal?"

"The big deal is I'm so far behind!" I cry.

"I doubt that. Melony said you were doing great."

I huff, not sure what to say. "Well, I feel behind. The girls are doing an intrasquad on Wednesday and I'm the only one not participating because I don't have routines."

"Paige, we knew this would be a push. You decided to fast track and go straight from Level 5 to Level 6. One month ago you thought you were going to be in Level 5 another year. Give yourself a break. Be realistic," she adds.

Be realistic. I think about that silently as we drive. Jason changes the subject back to himself and tells us that he did a magic trick at recess. He's not supposed to bring his magic supplies to school, but clearly he did. My mom must not be listening too closely to him because she hasn't gotten mad at him yet.

"Let's talk to Melony or Katie, or whoever we need to after practice today, okay? See what they think. If they think you need to stay maybe we can work something out."

"And make all of you miss the farm? That's not fair!" I yell.

"Paige, you are testing my patience."

I slump in my seat, "Sorry." I say. I really am sorry. I want to go to the farm and enjoy Thanksgiving. I also really want to learn my floor routine so I can catch up.

"How far away is the farm?" I ask, thinking maybe we can go back and forth.

"Two and a half hours," she says, giving me a

sideways glance that says, 'I am not driving you to practice that far away.' "Let's just see what Melony says about your routine today."

"Okay," I agree.

"Maybe we should have talked to your coaches sooner. I didn't really know what to expect when you started training with the optionals group. I didn't know you would want to do the intrasquad. It all seems so fast."

"Yeah," I agree. "I think that's why some kids, like Marissa, are waiting until next season to do Level 6."

"How are Savannah, Lucy, and Alexis dealing with it?" she asks me.

"They all scored out before I did, so they had time to learn floor and beam routines. Honestly the skills aren't a big change from Level 5 to Level 6. I think they'll be ready on Wednesday," I explain.

"So it's mostly the routines that you need to learn?" she asks trying to understand.

"I forgot my cards at school! Turn back!" Jason yells.

"Jason, I told you not to bring your magic toys to school," my mom chides.

"Turn back, please!" he begs.

"They'll be there tomorrow. And if they're not, then that's a good lesson for you to leave that stuff at home," she says, unbothered by the crying that has started in the back seat.

I can't stand it! "I have an old deck," I tell him.

His crying stops, "You do?"

"Yes. You can play with it tonight," I promise him.

"You spoil him," my mom whispers to me as the wailing stops.

Maybe. I need him to be on my side if I ask my parents not to go to the farm this weekend.

Chapter 10

At practice that night we start on beam. After a short complex we are assigned five stuck routines and then work B skills with any left-over time. Katie calls me over, presumably to give me my non-routine assignment.

"The intrasquad is tomorrow. Obviously you will not be able to do beam or floor since you don't have routines yet. But you can do vault and bars if you would like?"

I see she is waiting for me to answer, "I don't have a bar routine either," I point out.

"You can just do the Level 5 bar routine without the tap swings or the baby giant. You can add a sole circle or something if you want."

"I . . . I've never done a flyaway out of a cast," I remind her.

"You did it in the pit on to a mat last week didn't you?"

"Yeah, the pit. Not on the competition set."

"You are just off of season, which means you're still conditioned for a full bar routine. Just do a small cast into the dismount and I can spot you through the flyaway," she reasons.

I'm silent so she adds, "Or James can spot you."

"He'll be there?" I ask hopefully.

"He coaches compulsories on Wednesday, but I'm sure he can come over and spot you. And he coaches you guys on bars today as soon as the 3s are done with practice. You can try it then. I know you're used to James and that I'm pushing you pretty fast." I don't say anything so she finally wraps up her crazy idea with, "We can see how today goes and then decide."

"Okay," I agree.

"And your Tsuk entry is a no-brainer. You can do that tomorrow."

"Yeah," I agree. That I can do. One event. I guess that's better than nothing.

"Stick five back extension rolls, leaps, jumps, turns on high beam and then stick five round-offs," she instructs, abruptly turning my attention back to beam.

I nod and move to go to a beam that is open. "Oh and Paige," she calls back to me. I turn and wait. "Melony said she has a beam and floor routine for you. If you're in town you can learn both this weekend."

I don't know what to say so I nod and continue to the

beam and jump up. *If I'm in town.* Do I ask my family to stay in town just for me? That seems crazy and Jason would never forgive me. He loves the farm and the horses and our cousins. So do I.

I reach up and do a back extension roll and, shockingly, I stick it. I could rarely make these a few weeks ago. But I made it at State Championships and something clicked. I can make them a lot now.

"Those are so pretty," Brooklyn comments from the end of the beam where she is waiting for a turn.

"Thanks," I say and step up to do another one.

"I've never seen anyone except you do those on beam," she adds.

"That's because most people can do a back walkover," I remind her, but I am secretly happy with her compliment.

It takes me almost the entire work out to stick five of everything. I feel good about all of my beam skills. All I need to do is string together my skills with some dance and I'll be ready for the next intrasquad.

After beam we rotate to floor and, like beam, everyone is asked to do one full routine, two dance throughs with runs (for conditioning) and three of each pass. Katie has to call me over again for my own assignment.

"Four of each tumbling pass and three of each leap pass and your one and a half turn."

"Um, Katie?"

"What are my tumbling passes?" I ask, feeling super dumb, but I really don't know. I can't do bounders yet, or my layout. I'm not sure if that means I can't compete floor until I get those skills or if I compete easier passes that I can already do.

New Challenges

"Round-off back handspring layout or tuck for your back pass and front tuck for your front pass," she answers.

"Front tuck? I can do just the tuck for an entire pass?" I ask.

"You can. I'd like you to get that bounder as soon as possible, but the front alone is fine for now," she explains.

"It seems easier than Level 5," I point out.

"In some ways it is. Some kids don't stay in Level 6 very long," she comments.

I watch Lucy tumble by with a huge layout, "Like Lucy," I comment.

"Like Lucy," she confirms.

"Look Paige, you are going to do fine in Level 6 once you get your routines. James says you catch on to dance faster than most kids. You'll be doing routines just fine. You basically have all of your skills. We just need to get that layout on bars and floor and you are good to go."

"It just feels so close," I admit.

"I know we are pushing you fast, but it's that or wait an entire year and I think that you would get bored," she shares. I nod in agreement. "Work bounders after you're done with your assignment." With that I know she is done talking and needs to spot some of the girls on their tumbling passes.

I get started with warming up my layout pass first. I start with back tucks and when I am ready to do the layout I ask Katie to spot. I've never had Katie spot me before and I am nervous. I stand on the corner and tell myself it is exactly like having James spot. Except she is so much smaller. Can she really bump me up the way James does? I run and do a round-off back handspring back tuck. I feel

Katie bump me and I go way higher and rotate much faster than usual. I'm not ready for the landing. I can feel Katie grab my waist to help me on the landing, but I have too much rotation. She sets me down and I fall back to my bum with a bounce.

"I thought you said you were doing a layout," she says confused.

"I did. I meant to," I stammer as I stand up.

"You have to commit to a skill before you go or you'll hurt something," she says.

"Okay, I promise," and she nods and turns to her next tumbler. I'm just glad she doesn't know that I changed it because she was the one spotting.

I do my front tuck in the other diagonal and my leap pass along the edge of the floor. Then I stop and wait while Aubrey does a floor routine.

The 7s seem to know her routine and know when they can leap or tumble around her.

"Sixes, watch and learn her routine so you don't have to stop while she is going!" Katie yells out to all of us.

When Aubrey is done, it's my turn to do another layout. Katie sees me in the corner and motions for me to go. I know she knows she needs to spot me but since she doesn't do the hand motions like James I yell, "Layout?"

She nods and motions again. I know I can't stand here all day. Girls are standing behind me waiting to tumble. I take a deep breath and decide to do it this time for real.

I run, do a round-off back handspring, set, and pull my toes instead of my knees. I feel Katie bump me and I try to stay in a tight hollow position. I see the ground and feel her catch me just before I land.

"Beautiful Paige!" she says as soon as I land. I grin; it felt good! "Keep doing it like that and you will be doing them on your own in no time," she adds.

"Thanks," I say. I'm able to finish my floor assignment and I'm relieved I don't have to have the bounder to be able to compete. I think I may actually be able to pull off Level 6 this winter.

After floor we head up to the optionals room to put on our grips. It's still weird to go upstairs and walk past the Kip Club Cubbies. I see Trista, Carmen, and Marissa's names and I'm little sad to not be on the same team as them this season. I look up at the optionals door and remember that Level 6 and 7 train together, so likely we will all be together again next year.

We go to our lockers and have a quick snack as we pull on our grips.

"Are you going to try your flyaway without the taps?" Lucy asks me as she opens her locker door.

I feel my stomach tighten, "I don't know. I mean, I want to do something besides vault. I just don't feel ready," I admit.

"This gym is more about pushing you than waiting for you to be good and ready," she points out.

"Good and ready sounds nice right about now," I pout.

"Trust me, sometimes waiting stinks, too."

"Yeah, I guess so," I concede.

She shuts her locker door and has one grip on and the other in her hand. "On the flyaway, just do a tiny cast and pretend it's your third tap swing. It only gets scary when you do a giant cast into it. A big cast is harder to control."

"Pretend it's my third tap swing," I repeat.

"It worked for me when I was first doing them," she says pulling on her second grip.

"She's right," Brooklyn jumps in. "Do a small cast at first. Katie will throw you through it if you don't have enough height."

"So you're doing vault and bars tomorrow?" Savannah asks.

"Vault for sure. I'm undecided on bars," I tell her.

"You'll catch up," is all she says as she puts her empty grip bag in her locker. "Especially on floor and beam."

I don't know what to say to her vote of confidence, but I appreciate it. Maybe I will catch up on floor and beam once I have routines. The girls start filing downstairs to go to bars. I'm excited, nervous, and not at all sure how my bar workout is going to go.

After practice Melony has called the new Level 6s, Alexis, Savannah, Lucy, and I, into her office to order competition leotards. I'm giddy as I walk in. I did my flyaway out of a cast. Okay, it was a baby teeny tiny cast, but still I swung down and let go. Thankfully James was coaching bars because I was much more likely to go for it with him. I am starting to trust Katie, but maybe not enough for my first flyaway out of a cast. Anyway, I did it! As long as James spots me in the intrasquad on Wednesday I will be fine.

"Okay, girls, Katie is busy coaching the upper optional team so she asked me to help her order comp leos for you. These are the child large," she says pointing to a pile of long sleeve leotards sitting on her desk. "These are adult extra small," she gestures to a few laid over her chair, "and this one is adult small, which probably only Paige needs to try this one." I look up when I hear my name. Why am I being singled out as needing the biggest size? Then I look at my young teammates. They are only fifth graders, of course I'll need a bigger size. Still, I feel so large these days.

"Try on what you think is the best fit and I want to see it before we order," she instructs.

Alexis, Savannah, and Lucy grab for the first two piles and I grab the one adult small to see how it will fit. I don't remember what size my last leo was. I think a child large, but come to think of it, it was getting pretty tight.

"Are optionals still getting the leo with the one snowflake on the side?" Savannah asks.

"Yes, Levels 6, 7, and 8 get that one; 9s and 10s change every couple of years. They've worked hard to get where they are so we like to let them switch it up more."

Savannah nods and then we all file out to go up to the locker rooms to try on our sample leos. I listen to the three of them try on one size and then swap and try on another and then trade back again.

I'm standing in my adult small that fits perfectly, ready to go down and show Melony. "You guys better decide on something to go show Melony," I say.

I watch them swap sizes again and finally they are ready to go down with me. The sample leotards are black on the bottom with swirls on top. In my opinion, they aren't nearly as pretty as the Perfect Balance snowflake leos.

When we get to the bottom of the stairs and walk into the office, Savannah's mom is there talking to Melony.

"Hi girls!" she greets us. "Don't you four look darling in those leos!" she exclaims.

"Come over here so I can see," Melony instructs us. We walk over and she immediately says to me, "That looks perfect Paige. How does it feel?"

"Good. Better than my old one," I admit.

"Is it the small or extra small?" she asks in front of everyone.

"Small," I croak feeling so much bigger than my teammates.

Melony jots my size down on a piece of paper and moves over to tiny Lucy. "This may be a little baggy on you. What size is it?" she asks her.

"The child large," Lucy says, making me feel gigantic.

Thankfully Savannah's mom, Debbie, turns to me, "I hear you're getting your floor routine this weekend."

"Maybe. Well, I don't know," I stammer.

"Melony says it's done. I imagine you will want to learn it as soon as possible," she points out. She's not wrong. That would be best.

"We might be going out of town," I share.

Her eyes widen, "Really? When you are trying to pull together four new routines in six weeks?"

"Mom," I hear Savannah say to her mom in a warning tone.

"What? I'm not trying to be rude. It's a lot for anyone." Then she turns to me, "Paige, honey, if you want to stay with Savannah and I over the holiday we would love to have you. I can bring you here Friday, Saturday, Sunday, whatever you need," she offers.

"Really?" I ask, surprised at her generosity. "What about Thanksgiving?" I ask.

"Oh, don't worry about the holiday. It's just going to be Savannah, me, and Savannah's grandma. You would make it a perfect four. We do a simple turkey dinner and watch movies."

I stand there thinking about it. It would be great to learn my routine this weekend. Then again, I would be bummed not to be with my family for Thanksgiving or my birthday. I'm pretty sure my birthday falls on Thanksgiving weekend this year. I need to ask my mom.

"Melony, when would you be able to work with Paige?" Debbie asks.

Melony is examining Alexis' leo and absently responds with, "Any day except Thursday," she says, tugging Alexis' sleeve.

"You can do Sunday, right?" Debbie asks, knowing that some people in Utah don't work on Sunday.

"Yep, Sunday is fine. Alexis you are between sizes so let's size up to the adult extra small."

Debbie turns to me and says, "You could work on it a couple of times!"

I nod, warming up to the idea.

"Talk to your mom and let me know," Debbie says when I don't say anything.

"Okay," I agree.

My mom and Alexis' mom both come into the office and Melony starts talking to them about our new competition leotards. Mainly they are discussing price and Melony takes their credit cards. A few minutes later Lucy's mom comes in and Melony goes through the entire process with her.

"Custom leotards usually take six weeks. If they are late the girls can start the season in their Level 5 leos."

As the girls and moms select sizes, Melony makes a note of what she is going to order each girl. When it's my turn to make a decision with my mom Melony jots down my size and then looks up. "I have a floor routine for Paige. Are you guys in town this weekend so she can learn it?" she asks my mom.

"We are out of town this weekend."

"I told Paige she can stay with me," Debbie offers, jumping into the conversation. She sees my mom's confused expression and explains more. "I can take her to the gym Friday and Saturday to work on it. Sunday if she needs it."

My mom turns and looks at me questioningly. I don't know what to say so I give a little shrug. "That's a very sweet offer, Debbie," my mom says. "We'll talk about it as a family tonight." That answer seems to satisfy Debbie and the moms go back to talking about a book McKell, Lucy's mom, was telling them about.

When we finally get out of the gym and into the car my mom instantly says, "You don't want to miss the farm, do you?"

"I don't know," I admit.

"You love the farm," she says quietly.

"I know," I agree.

"Your birthday is on Friday this year," she says.

"It is?" I ask. That makes missing the farm so much worse.

"You are okay missing both?"

"I don't know," I say, feeling so very conflicted.

CHAPTER 11

After a lot of deliberation, and my dad going nuts that I would consider missing Thanksgiving, we finally come up with a compromise. We are all going out to the farm today after practice as originally planned. We will have Thanksgiving tomorrow with Aunt Jennifer and Uncle Justin's family, play on the farm Friday and Saturday, and then Saturday afternoon my mom and I are going to drive back to Snowcap Canyon. I will work on my routine with Melony on Sunday morning. I'll get to be with my family for my birthday before my mom and I come back early.

Melony said the Level 6 routines are short and I could

probably learn it in one day. I'm happy with this compromise because I get the best of both situations. I get to spend most of Thanksgiving at the farm and still get my floor routine over the weekend.

Today is an easy workout since we are doing the practice intrasquad. There are no judges today, just Katie. It's still stressful to do new routines in front of all of your teammates. I feel a little lame that I am only doing two events.

We aren't competing in Olympic order like we would at a meet. We're rotating how we normally would in practice, which means beam first. While my teammates warm up on the high beams Katie tells me to work on my skills on low beam.

"Oh, Paige, I was thinking about you last night. If you don't get your round-off on high beam you're going to need a series. Try handstands right into your back extension roll."

"I thought I could just do my back extension roll if I don't get a round-off," I say, confused.

"It's not a flight skill. You need either a series or a flight element," she quickly explains and turns back to her athletes warming up on high beam.

I need a series or a skill in flight. Optionals is complicated. How would I do a handstand into a back extension roll? I decide to try it on the out-of-bounds line along the edge of the floor. I kick up into a handstand, then I step down making sure to step down with my feet together so I can go right into my back extension roll. My back extension roll is a mess, but I connected it. I try again, this time making sure the handstand is straight so my back extension roll is straight. Almost! This is kind of fun.

I do a few more and Katie tells me to take them to low beam. I nod and go to a low beam that already has panel mats on either side of it. I do the handstand just in front of the panel mats so my back extension roll is at the mats. It's much harder than on the line on the floor. I sigh, this is going to be as hard as the round-off.

Before I'm able to do another one Katie calls us over to give us our order for routines. Of course, she does not name me since I'm not doing a routine. I know I am expected to sit and watch my teammates perform their routines.

We all sit in a row on a low beam facing the high beams. Riley is waiting by a high beam to salute Katie. I watch as she salutes and begins her routine. I notice she does a back walkover back handspring. A series and a flight skill. I wonder why she isn't Level 7. Maybe another event is holding her back.

I watch the rest of the Level 6s closely to see what they have in their routines. Riley and Victoria, the two returning Level 6s, both do a back walkover back handspring. Alexis and Savannah both do a back handspring and Lucy does a back walkover back walkover. Lucy will replace that series with a back handspring soon.

Aubrey, Brooklyn, Peyton, and Maya, the Level 7s, all do a back handspring series. I'm definitely the outlier doing back extension rolls and round-offs. On the one hand I think it's kind of cool my routine will be different. On the other hand, I understand it means my skills are harder. I don't have a lot of choice; my shoulders will just not allow my hands to get close enough for a back walkover or back handspring on beam.

Katie comes over and talks to us about how the beam rotation went. There were several falls and she talks about how we just need to 'put in the numbers' meaning we have to do a lot of routines in practice so we don't fall in meets. Then she tells us to grip up for bars.

I head upstairs with my teammates to get my grips. I'm extremely nervous for bars. I look out the parent viewing window as we pass it to get our grips. I see James on floor with the Level 4s and 5s and I hope I can pull him away to spot me on bars.

I need to remember to do a small cast and pretend it's the third tap swing like in Level 5. I remind myself this over and over as I get my grips on and follow my team back downstairs. We warm up with push away kips as usual. Then we each do a first half, last half, and one routine.

When I am ready for my last half I ask Katie if I can call James over to spot me on the flyaway. She nods and then yells over to him. Melony is coaching with him so he can leave for a moment.

He comes over to the bars, stands under the high bar, and nods to me. "Out of the cast?" he asks, double checking what he is spotting. "Yes, out of the cast. No baby giant, just kip, cast, flyaway," I answer.

"Piece of cake," he says, stepping closer to the high bar. I kip, squat on, jump to the high bar, and do my long hang kip. *Small cast*, I think as I cast out of the kip and push away to swing down into the fly away. *Just like the third tap swing.* When I see my toes come up I let go and I feel James' hand on my back as he bumps me up harder than usual. Even with the bump I barely make it around to my feet. I land short and take a few huge steps forward.

"That was a little too small," James comments.

"But too big makes the tap swing feel out of control," I counter.

"Too small and you won't make it around," he points out. I sigh and nod. "You'll find the sweet spot. Call me over on your full set," he says and walks back over to floor. I watch him go and feel dumb that I have to have him come over here at all. I should be able to have Katie spot. Not today though. Today is enough new stuff and Katie doesn't seem to mind.

When it's my turn again, Katie calls over to James. He trots over and asks, "Full set?" I nod and he gets into place under the high bar. He motions for me to go. I begin my very basic Level 6 routine. Kip, free hip, kip, squat on, jump to high bar, long hang kip. I'm too nervous to cast bigger like James said, so I cast about the same as last time and I do a flyaway about the same as last time, too.

After I take my huge step forward James says, "Fix it next week. For today you are good enough to do a routine in the intrasquad." I smile with relief.

"Paige, you're fourth up," Katie says to me.

"Okay," I agree and walk over to the chalk tray. I watch as the rest of my teammates finish warming up. I start getting nervous as I stand and wait.

"Let's have you guys sit over here," Katie says gesturing to a panel mat sitting on the floor near the bars.

"Can I pull one more over?" Maya asks and Katie nods.

We all sit in a row on two panel mats and I see

Savannah is first and Lucy is chalking up. I watch as Savannah does the same routine as I do with higher casts, clear hips, and a strong layout flyaway. Then Lucy does the same routine, only she pops up to handstand on her casts using the straddle up way James taught her.

Then Katie and Aubrey move the bars slightly farther apart for Riley, Victoria, Alexis, and I. Alexis does a clean routine and then it's my turn. As soon as James is ready Katie salutes me.

"You've got this, Paige!" I hear someone, maybe Maya, yell as I salute back. I'm glad I get to do this routine. I jump into my kip and begin. I do a clean kip, clear hip, kip, squat on. I don't even hit my feet on floor as I swing under for my second kip. I jump to the high bar and swing into a long hang kip and start thinking about my cast. *Not too big, not too small.* I cast a little higher than I meant to, but I'm able to pike my body and slow down my swing a little. *Third tap*, I tell myself and when my feet come up, I let go. I can feel James spot me lighter than before, but I land just fine. I finish and turn to salute Katie. Then I look up at James to see him beaming.

He gives me a high five, "Nice Red."

He tips an imaginary hat to Katie and runs back over to his Level 4s and 5s.

I did it! I walk over to sit on the panel mat and Victoria gives me a quick high five as she passes me to the chalk tray. I sit down and Savannah whispers to me, "That was a great flyaway."

"Thanks shrimp," I say, using an old nick name. I notice it makes her a little red and I realize maybe I should ditch that nick name and just call her Anna like everyone else.

I see Katie salute Riley and I watch as she does our same routine, only she swings almost to handstand out of her casts and clear hip. And, of course, her flyaway is a layout. Victoria's routine is similar.

Then we watch the Level 7s. Their routines are similar except they have added giants. That looks like a really difficult skill and I'm glad I have at least another year before I have to worry about it.

Brooklyn finishes out our rotation with a beautiful bar routine complete with giants and stalder swings. We are told to put our grips away and go to vault. I'm happy that I'm doing vault and bars today. At least I'm doing half the events which feels a little more like I belong here than just doing one event. Mostly, I'm happy bars is over and all I have left to do is a half-on entry. Then I can sit back and watch my teammates' floor routines.

We quickly warm up vault with two sprints and two vaults. Then Katie puts us in order by size and vault so moving the equipment is easier for her. This puts Alexis and Savannah first. They don't seem to mind as they both do half-ons, or Tsuk timers. I know both of them are working Yurchenkos, but that is a harder entry and my guess is they're not ready yet.

I do my half-on after Alexis and then we watch Lucy and the returning Level 6s and the Level 7s all do Yurchenko entries. That vault looks crazy hard and I'm glad my shoulders make it so I never have to do that vault. For once, I'm grateful for my impossibly tight shoulders.

The girls are excited as we rotate to floor. Floor is where optionals is really fun. I'm familiar with my

New Challenges

teammates' routines by now, but it will still be fun to sit and watch them.

"Paige, I want you to work back tucks and front tucks while they warm up," Katie instructs. I nod and join my teammates in the corner of the diagonal. They have been instructed to do two of each pass. I will tumble until the rest of my team is ready to compete.

I get in three of each pass before the rest of the team is ready. Katie tells us where to sit and the girls line up in order of competition. I sit at the very end since I'm not competing. As I watch Alexis walk onto the floor and wait to start her routine I feel better than I did during beam. I successfully did two routines today. More than that, I know when I get a floor routine, I will be a strong Level 6 on floor. I'm good at dance and floor has always been my best event. I wonder what Melony has come up with as I watch Alexis' pretty Beauty and the Beast routine.

Alexis finishes and Riley pops up. I watch Riley, Victoria, and Savannah closely. All of their routines are very different and I'm pretty sure Melony created all of them. She's good. She knows how to tailor the routine to the individual girl. I can't wait to learn mine on Sunday. I happily watch the Level 7s perform. Like Level 6, their routine is only two tumbling passes. The big difference is that their tumbling passes are harder.

"Do they have the same routine as last season?" I ask Riley who is sitting next to me on the other side of Alexis.

"Yes, we keep the same routines for Level 6 and 7. Of course, they change for Level 8 because upper optional routines are so much longer," she explains.

"They look good," I add.

"Yeah, they're ready," she agrees.
That is what I need. To be ready.

Chapter 12

As soon as practice is over I hurry out of the gym as quickly as possible. My family is driving to my aunt's farm tonight and we are going straight from my practice. I jump in the car and my brother thoughtfully hands me my tablet.

"Thanks," I say, taking it from him. It's not that my tablet is that important to me, but it's the ultimate gift from my brother. He loves video games and since my mom limits his time each day, he loves road trips.

"We can play the entire drive," he reminds me. I nod and try to hide my grin.

I buckle up next to Jason and notice my mom isn't in the front with my dad. "Where's Mom?" I ask.

"She went up early since we needed to drive two cars anyway," my dad replies.

"Why do we need two cars?" I ask.

He glances at me in the mirror and says, "So you can go back early on Saturday."

"Oh," I say, feeling bad I'm inconveniencing my parents so much. "Can I have something to eat?" I ask him.

"Right here," he says, passing a plastic container back to me. I open it up and find my mom's fancy macaroni and cheese. I breath in the smell and realize it's still pretty warm. It's a little messy in the car but I manage by holding it up under my chin. I am starving. Why am I so hungry? I can't seem to get the food in fast enough.

"How was the intrasquad?" my dad asks.

"Good," I say around a mouthful of food.

"Did you do vault and bars?" he asks, knowing that bars was a maybe going into the day. I nod since I'm chewing. Without a word he hands me a bottle of water and I take a long drink.

"I'm so hungry!" I exclaim.

"I see that. Maybe we need to send you with a bigger snack," he suggests and I nod in agreement. "You're growing," he comments with pride.

"When do we get there?" I ask.

My dad chuckles, "That's supposed to be Jason's line." I look over at Jason engrossed in his game and I know I won't hear a peep from him until we get there. "The weather is clear so it should only take us a couple of hours," my dad answers. When I don't say anything he adds, "Mom said they have a big surprise for you for your birthday." I love when my birthday falls on the holiday weekend. I get to spend my birthday with my cousins. It's like a 4-day birthday party instead of one afternoon.

"I wonder what it is," I comment.

"Thirteen is a big deal. I bet Jennifer went all out," my dad guesses.

I smile thinking about that as I finish the last of the pasta. I set the container at my feet. Then I lean back in my seat and look around. I guess I can't read because it's dark. I pick up my tablet and plug in my earphones. I decide to listen to music and watch the videos. As I relax into the seat I feel extremely tired. I find myself unable to keep my eyes open any longer.

When I wake up I'm in the car and Jason is still playing games next to me.

"Are we almost there?" I ask.

"Yes, only about five minutes," my dad answers.

We arrive only a few minutes later. I get out of the car and start grabbing bags while my dad has to break the news to Jason that we arrived and he has to stop playing games.

My aunt bursts open the door and my cousins come flying out behind her. I see my mom step out onto the porch, happy to see we made it. Chloe and Noah barrel toward us for hugs, Grace is a teenager so she hangs back and waits for the commotion to die down before she greets us.

At age eleven, Chloe is a year and a half younger than me. Noah is the youngest at age nine, a bit older than Jason. They hug all of us before we can get to the steps of the house.

I look up at my Aunt Jennifer and Uncle Justin on the steps of their idyllic farmhouse. It's white with a porch that

New Challenges

wraps all the way around it. Since it's dark all we can see are the front steps, the front door, and a swing just to the right of the door. But I know from coming here before that the deck wraps all the way around and there is nothing but fields on all sides with a view of the massive Rocky Mountains from the back.

"Welcome to the J&J Ranch," my aunt says, giving me a hug. "You've grown!" she exclaims stepping back to take a look at me. We haven't seen them since early summer. I haven't grown that much since then, have I?

I hug her back and when she moves to Jason I greet Grace. She is a year older than me and she has fiery red hair like mine, only hers is straight. Our parents loved to take pictures of us together when we were babies because the color of our hair was so similar to each other and unusual from everyone else.

"Hi Grace," I greet.

"Hey," she says without much emotion. I don't take offense to Grace's greeting. She is shy. She likes horses better than people. By tomorrow she'll be talking. Once she remembers she likes us.

"Let me help you with your bags," Uncle Justin says, going to our car and lifting bags out.

"Grace, show the kids to the bonus room," Aunt Jennifer instructs.

Whenever we are here all the kids sleep on the floor in the bonus room. Not that there isn't enough room in their bedrooms, we just like to all be together. I grab my bag and follow Grace even though I know exactly where to go.

Once we are settled in the bonus room and my parents are settled in the guest room, Aunt Jennifer invites us down for milk and cookies before bed. This is an unusual treat for Jason and I and we immediately accept.

There's a lot of chattering going on in the kitchen at once. My mom asks me about the intersquad and I fill her in on my two events. My dad is talking with my aunt and uncle about their new horse, Noah is talking to my brother about doing archery tomorrow, and Chloe starts telling me about new kittens.

"New kittens?" I ask, perking up.

"Yeah, sometimes the cats have a litter in the fall. It's rough on the babies, but they are in the barn, so they should make it through the winter."

"How many?" I ask.

"Five."

"I'd love to see them," I say.

"Tomorrow," her mom interjects. "You can feed them at first light."

"How did she know what we were talking about?" I ask.

"She hears everything," Grace answers. "Best to be quiet." I look at Grace and nod. Maybe that's why she likes to be quiet.

"What is new with you?" I ask Grace.

"Eighth grade sucks. But other than that, the new horse, Marshmallow, is cool."

"I can't wait to see her," I say, sincerely.

"It sounds like you guys have a big day planned. Finish up your cookies and let's get to bed."

I finish my cookies, put my milk cup in the sink, and follow the kids upstairs. I'm used to just Jason and I in the house. The five of us feels a little chaotic.

New Challenges

By the time we get in our jammies, teeth brushed, and sleeping bags out I'm exhausted. The boys have decided to sleep in Noah's room, probably so they can sneak games, which is fine by me. I'll have time to catch up with Chole and Grace.

"How's gymnastics?" Chloe asks, fluffing her pillow and settling in for the night.

"Good. Hard, but good. I'm in a new Level now," I share.

"That's cool. It looks scary. Is it scary?" she asks.

"Sometimes," I admit. But then I think about the sport they are into and I add, "No scarier than jumping horses I suppose."

They both like this comment as we lay down in our bags. We are too tired to say much more.

"Kittens in the morning," Chloe reminds me.

"Kittens in the morning," I agree. "Good night."

They both say good night and I quietly look up at the ceiling. I'm glad I didn't stay back with Savannah and her mom. Being here and thinking about something else for a moment feels good.

Chapter 13

I wake up to light streaming in through the front windows of the house. The bonus room is empty. Chloe and Grace must be up.

I get up and rummage through my bag to find fleece lined jeans and a waffle long sleeve shirt. I know I'll be outside today. I also know it will be cold. After I dress I head downstairs to a bustling kitchen. My mom and Aunt Jennifer are busy preparing for our Thanksgiving dinner.

"Happy Thanksgiving, pumpkin!" my mom exclaims when she sees me.

I rub my eyes and mumble Happy Thanksgiving back. "Where is everyone?" I ask.

"The dads are feeding the horses, the boys are feeding the dogs, and the girls are waiting for you to go feed the kittens."

"Oh. I'm last up?" I ask, a little embarrassed.

"You must have needed the sleep. Your mom has been telling me how hard you've been working on your gymnastics."

"It has gotten hard, but I like it. Where are the girls waiting?"

"They're on the front porch swinging. No rush; have some breakfast first. Those kittens can wait," she says, handing me a bowl of oatmeal with apples cut up and cinnamon sprinkled on top. "You can take that outside," she says.

I take the bowl and spoon she is offering me and walk out the front door onto the porch. To the left Chloe and Grace are swinging on the bench swing.

"You're going too fast; I'm going to spill!" Grace exclaims.

"Morning," I say, startling them and hopefully breaking up the fight that is brewing.

"Morning," Grace says jumping up. "Let's sit over here Paige."

"No," Chloe whines, "I won't pump too fast, I promise!"

"There's not room for three anyway. We can sit on the rocking chairs or stairs," Grace decides.

Chloe sticks out her lower lip and swings her legs up onto the bench so she is taking up the entire thing. I walk over and sit in a rocking chair while Grace takes the one next to me.

"I can't wait to meet the kittens. Have you named them all?" I ask Chloe.

This brightens up her mood and she straightens, "I've only named one Peek-a-boo because he likes to play peek-a-boo. The mom is named Mama because she always seems to have kittens. I'm waiting to learn the personalities of the others before I name them."

"Can I name one?" I ask.

Chloe thinks for a minute and says, "Only if the one you name likes you."

"Fair enough," I decide and dig into my oatmeal.

After we're done eating we take our dishes into the kitchen. Aunt Jennifer hands us two cans of kitten food and we head to the barn.

We walk across the yard and it's bitter cold even though the sun is out. It looks like a beautiful day, but the air has an arctic breeze. Without a word, all of us walk a little faster.

When we enter the barn the horses sense us and whiney their greetings. The girls say hi to each of them by name as they pass their stalls. When we get to the other end of the barn there's a ladder leaned against the wall heading up to the loft. Chloe scrambles up the ladder and I follow her with Grace behind me.

The loft has hay bales stacked everywhere and a small path to walk. I hear faint meowing in the far left corner. Chloe skips the path forward and heads left where there's a small space to walk. She knows exactly where Mama is located. I follow Chloe and sure enough in the back corner curled against a bale of hay is the mama cat with several kittens around her. Some are nursing and some are wandering around crying in a high-pitched meow.

"Oh my gosh, they're so cute!" I exclaim.

"You should have seen them a few weeks ago," Grace comments, sitting down next to the mama cat. "Hi Mama," she says. The cat looks up in acknowledgement of our greeting. She doesn't seem to mind we are there.

"She knows you guys?" I ask.

"Of course," Chloe says, setting out bowls spaced several inches apart. Then she hands me a can and a fork, "Here scoop one out and the kittens will come running." I take the can from her and scoop the mushy stinky kitten food into a bowl. Sure enough as soon as the kittens hear the sound of my spoon scooping the food into the bowl they come running. They smoosh all their heads into the bowl as they frantically eat. They're so crowded I can't finish putting food in the bowl.

"Greedy little guys," I say laughing.

"If you fill this bowl we can move some of them over here so they aren't so crowded," she comments.

I move over to the second bowl and I'm able to empty out the can in that bowl without any of the kittens even noticing. Once I'm done Chloe grabs one of them and sets her by the second bowl. I do the same with a sweet little black one.

I watch them as they eat. There are three tortoiseshell kittens, one that is all black, and one that is white with black tipped ears and black fur around her blue eyes. I reach down and pet them while they eat.

"You haven't named four of them?" I ask.

"They've been hard to tell apart so I was waiting to watch their personalities. That way I know who is who later."

"They're probably old enough to name now," Grace says.

"Should we stay and play with them?" Chloe asks.

Grace shrugs, "If we go back to the house mom is going to make us peel potatoes."

Chloe smiles, "Naming them it is then." She reaches over and pulls a few pieces of hay out of a bale and hands us each one. I take mine wondering why she gave it to me. I don't say anything; I just twirl it between my fingers.

The black kitten walks away from the bowl and Grace immediately starts swishing her piece of hay back and forth on the ground in front of the kitten and she immediately pounces on it making us laugh. When another kitten is done eating Chloe does the same. They are so curious and playful.

The white kitten stops eating and walks toward me. I move my piece of straw back and forth just how Chloe and Grace did. The white kitten doesn't pounce like her siblings. She squats down behind a bale of hay, peeks her head around the corner, and watches my piece of straw from a safe distance.

"Am I doing it wrong?" I ask.

Chloe looks up from playing with the two kittens to see who I am entertaining and says, "No, she's just a cautious one. Keep doing it. She'll play when she's had time to think about it." I do as she says and keep swiping my straw back and forth. I notice her eyes are following the straw closely. I slow it down a little to see what she'll do. Her face is focused and her ears are turned forward. I look over and Grace and Chloe both have two kittens playing

New Challenges

with them and I can't even get this one to engage. I look back at my cautious kitten and decide not to give up on her. I move the straw forward and back then side to side. I see her focus narrow in even more when I move the straw side to side. Then out of nowhere she pounces! She catches me off guard and pulls the piece of hay out of my hand.

"Hey! That's mine!" I exclaim trying to grab it back. She puts a paw on it to keep it in place.

"She's good when she decides to pounce," Chloe comments. "She's faster than the others."

"We can call her Flash," Grace comments.

"No, that's not good enough," I decide..

"Once you name enough animals, anything is good enough."

"I've never named an animal," I admit.

"Then you should do all of them!" Chloe exclaims.

I look up, "Really? You guys don't mind?"

"We have lots of chances, especially since we name the chickens."

"Okay," I agree looking over at the other four kittens playing with Chloe and Grace. "The black one should be Noche," I comment referring to the word night in Spanish.

"Night?" Grace says, getting it right away. I nod and look at the tortoiseshell kittens.

"They look like messy paintings. Maybe Picasso?" I muse.

"Or Sunset, to go with Noche," Chloe suggests.

I laugh, "That's so silly."

"Pet names can be super silly. Even horses."

"This little lady looks like a puff of snow," I say referring to my cautious kitten who is back to hiding behind a bale and watching me intently. "Snow Queen, Snowflake, Snowball, Snowfluff . . ." I muse out loud.

"I like Snow Queen or maybe even Snow Lady."

"You know she's not going to stay white, right?" Grace says.

"She's not?" I ask.

"No. She has the markings of a Siamese. We have a Siamese Tom around here that gives Mama a half Siamese kitten once in a while. Look at her blue eyes and black markings on her face and ears. Those are Siamese markings. Her coat will darken with age."

I pick her up from her hiding place and put her in my lap. She wanders around on my legs, not wanting to cuddle. I pet her snowy white fur and am sad that we all have to grow up and change. "That's too bad," I say stroking her.

"We have Peek-a-boo, Noche, Snow-something, what about this one?" Chloe asks, picking up another tortoiseshell-colored kitten.

"This is harder than I thought," I say laughing. "Should we let Jason name one?"

"Sure," Chloe says, setting her down.

"We should get back. Mom will be mad if we avoid chores for too long," Grace decides.

We agree and give all the kittens one last good-bye and head back down the ladder to the main level of the barn.

Grace was right. As soon as we walk back into the house Aunt Jennifer puts us to work peeling potatoes.

"Do the chickens need feeding?" Chloe asks hopefully.

"The boys are doing it," Aunt Jennifer comments.

"They'll be out there forever," Grace says, knowing their trick.

Aunt Jennifer doesn't say anything and just goes back to work on whatever dish she is making. I'm guessing she doesn't care how long they're gone as long as everyone is doing some kind of chore.

We work quietly for a while. The kitchen is warm and smells like Thanksgiving. The Turkey has been in the oven all morning and I watch as my mom opens the oven and bastes it.

My cousins and I are each sitting on a chair with a bucket in front of us and a pile of potatoes on the kitchen counter. We are peeling them over the bucket and then putting the peeled potatoes in a huge bowl sitting on the table.

"Do we seriously need all of these?" Grace complains.

"I like leftovers," Aunt Jennifer comments. "Plus potatoes always look like more before they're mashed."

"Can we go outside when this is done?" Chloe asks.

"Once you guys get most of the potatoes peeled you can go play and send the boys in. They're not going to get away with not doing kitchen chores on Thanksgiving."

This satisfies my cousins and we don't say anymore as we hunker down and peel potatoes. I notice the girls are faster than me. They've done this a lot more than I have. I think the last time I peeled potatoes was last Thanksgiving. I rarely help my mom in the kitchen and I'm a little embarrassed to admit it. I hope they don't see how slow and uncoordinated my peeling is compared to theirs.

I look over and watch Grace expertly rotate the potato around as she peels. I think I would get my finger in the blade if I did it like that. I'm finally done with my first potato and I put it in the giant bowl Aunt Jennifer set out. I notice three potatoes are already in there. My guess is that Grace already did two and Chloe one before I got one done. I try not to worry about it as I reach for a new one to peel.

"Shall we put on music?" My mom asks.

"Alexa, play holiday music," Aunt Jennifer commands. Instantly Christmas music comes on. This house is a weird combination of old and new. The animals, farm equipment, and the barn all seem out of the past. Yet Aunt Jennifer has technology in her house that we don't even have yet.

"Are we allowed to have Christmas music before Thanksgiving?" my mom teases.

"As far as I'm concerned, Thanksgiving is for getting together with family and kicking off the season."

"Does that mean we can get a tree tomorrow?" Chloe asks, setting down a peeled potato on the table and picking up another one.

"I think so. I'll have to double check if your dad got a permit," Aunt Jennifer comments as she dumps ingredients into her giant electric mixer and turns it on.

"What does he need a permit for?" I ask.

"For cutting down a tree in the mountains. They don't want them to be over harvested at the holidays so they give permits for certain areas. Some years we don't get one and have to go get our tree in town," Grace says wrinkling up her nose as if that is the most awful way to get a tree.

I laugh, "I take it you like the ones from the mountains."

"Yeah, they're the best."

"They smell so good," Chloe chimes in.

Our moms start talking about what they want to decorate tomorrow and it sounds like a lot. I enjoy listening to them planning along with the Christmas music in the background. Christmas at the farm is fun. I have some great memories here of snowed-in white Christmases.

My peaceful thoughts are broken by Jason and Noah slamming through the front door.

"Perfect timing!" Aunt Jennifer yells.

"We can't help. Jason just had to come in to pee!" Noah yells back as they run by. "And I'm getting my bows," he adds.

"Yeah, you girls will definitely have to tag them in when you get about halfway done," she decides.

At the mention of the restroom I decide I should go before we get the green light to be done with potatoes and can go outside. I set my potato down and head to the bathroom off the kitchen but realize Jason is in there so I head upstairs to Grace and Chloe's bathroom. I step in and shut and lock the door.

When I'm finished I go to wash my hands and the soap dispenser is completely empty. I look around for more soap, but that is the only dispenser in here. Mom keeps her extra soap under the sink; maybe Aunt Jennifer does too.

I crouch down and open the cupboard under the sink. I see two baskets under the sink and soap lined up to the right of the baskets. *Bingo*, I think as I reach for the soap. As I am grabbing the soap I notice that the basket is full of pads neatly lined up in yellow wrappers. Grace needs pads? I look at the basket next to it and it has colorful fabrics folded into little squares. I wonder what that is? I take one and as soon as I hold it up, I realize it is a pair of brightly patterned underwear. Embarrassed that I grabbed one of Grace's underwear I try to fold it back up just how I found it and put it back in the basket. Why does she have underwear in the bathroom?

I stand up with the soap, set it on the counter and begin to wash my hands. I can't decide if I'm insulted that I haven't gotten my period yet or glad. I feel like my friends all know something grown up that I don't know.

I head back downstairs wondering what getting your period is like. Abigail and Katherine talked about it a little, but I didn't feel like I could ask them questions. Maybe I could ask Grace. When I walk into the kitchen Grace and Chloe are gone and Noah and Jason are in their place.

"Where'd you go?" my mom asks.

"To the bathroom."

"Grace and Chloe headed back outside. The boys are going to do the rest."

I don't need any more explanation than that as I turn and grab my coat by the door and head outside. We play tag outside until we are called in for dinner.

Thankfully there's a kids table. Aunt Jennifer and Uncle Justin invited a bunch of adults over for dinner that don't have family in town. The adult table looks formal and intimidating. The kid's table is more fun, in my opinion. It's just the five of us and most of the time Jason entertains us with his off-the-wall jokes.

We are done much earlier than the adults and we're excused to go play. Since it gets dark early this time of year, we have to come up with something to do inside. We go up to the bonus room where our cousins teach us a made-up version of billiards. Instead of using pool sticks we just push the balls around with our hands. Since Noah seems to have established rules, he teaches them to us, and the game is pretty fun.

    When Noah is about to beat us all our parents call us down for pie. We run down the stairs and sit only long enough to eat warm homemade pie. Then we run back upstairs to start a movie and fall asleep altogether in the bonus room.

    It was a great Thanksgiving.

Chapter 14

The next morning I'm the last one to get up again. Which is a bit of a bummer since it's my birthday.

I head downstairs and when I walk into the kitchen there is the usual morning bustle but on the wall there is a banner that says, 'Happy Birthday!'

"Good morning birthday girl!" my aunt says coming over to give me a hug.

"Thanks," I say, happy she remembered.

"I love it when your birthday falls on Thanksgiving weekend and we get to celebrate with you," she exclaims.

"Is that my birthday girl?" I hear my mom say, coming in from the front porch.

"Hi Mom," I reply. She is bundled up from being outside. I'm guessing she was out there having a quiet cup of coffee.

"How's my teenager?" she exclaims.

I smile, "The same," I say. I really do feel the same.

"You are absolutely not the same," my aunt interjects. "Look how tall you are and filling out just like a lady." *Filling out?* What does that mean? I don't want to fill out. I want to be the same.

"Where are the others?" I ask.

"Noah and Chloe went to deliver some bales with Justin. Jason and Grace are feeding the horses."

"Can I feed the kittens?" I ask.

"You sure can. Breakfast first," she says, scooping scrambled eggs onto a plate for me.

I quietly eat and when I am almost done I ask, "Where's Dad?"

"On the porch reading. I think he's waiting to wish you a happy birthday," my mom says.

"Okay," I say and take the can of kitten food Aunt Jennifer has opened and is handing to me. I go to the door and pull on my boots. Then I put on my coat and decide to grab a beanie hat from the rack.

I walk outside and sure enough my dad is in one of the rocking chairs looking at his phone. He doesn't look up when I step out so I walk a little closer.

"Oh, hi pumpkin," he says, using my family nickname. "Are you too old for me to call you pumpkin?"

"No," I say, shaking my head. "I'm the same," I repeat.

"Well not entirely. You're thirteen today. Holy cow, when did I get so old that I have a teenager?"

I'm silent because I don't think I should agree with him that he's old. "We're going to have a great day," he decides. "Are you headed to feed the kittens?" he asks, seeing the can in my hand.

"Yeah, they're so cute, you should see them," I brighten a little.

"I can't get up that ladder," he teases. "You enjoy those kittens birthday girl," he says.

"Thanks Dad, I will."

I turn and walk down the porch steps and across the yard to the barn. It's another crisp day and I wonder how Mama and her kittens stand it. I get to the barn and find Grace teaching my brother how to feed the horses. For once he is being serious and calm. They turn when they hear me and Jason whispers, "Happy Birthday."

"Why are you whispering?" I ask.

"Because we are being quiet and calm," Grace says and winks at me. In that moment she looks just like my mom.

"Oh, got it," I whisper back. "I'm just going to feed Snow Queen and the rest of her court," I say heading to the ladder.

"Going with Snow Queen, huh? Even though she'll be darker in a few weeks?"

"I think so," I say as I head up the ladder awkwardly using the sides of my hands since one hand is carrying the can of kitten food and the other hand has a spoon and bowl. I finally make it up and head back to Mama's corner. Sure enough she is in the same spot she was yesterday and kittens are meowing around her. Mama must not ever get any sleep.

New Challenges

"Hi Mama," I greet her, setting down the bowl. "I'm here to give your little ones some extra food," I explain as I scoop food out of the can and kittens come dashing over.

"I'm not sure why they act so hungry. You seem to feed them just fine," I comment. She looks at me with the wisdom of a mother and sets her chin on her paws.

I sit down cross legged and pick up a piece of straw. All the kittens are busy eating the food I brought so I twirl it between my fingers while I wait. I can't believe I'm thirteen today. I don't feel thirteen, whatever that is supposed to feel like. All the other teenagers I know, like Grace, and even Abigail and Katherine, seem so much more sophisticated than I am. I hate that I'm growing so much. I didn't think it was that much, but it's all anyone can seem to talk about. I have noticed tumbling is harder. I wonder if my older Level 7 teammates, Brooklyn or Maya, went through a growth spurt too. I should get to know them. I feel like I've gotten thrown into this group so fast I haven't really gotten to know the other girls. That and I feel safe with Savannah, Alexis, and Lucy so I haven't talked much to my new teammates.

Snow Queen finishes her meal and walks toward me with curiosity. I swipe the straw on the ground in front of her and she cautiously watches it. Then her brothers and sisters join us until they are in each other's way and I decide to pick up a second straw and play with that one a little way away. They make me laugh as they stalk and pounce with very little coordination. Even funnier is how they run into each other. After a while Snow Queen retreats and climbs into my lap. I drop the straw to pet her. She purrs for a brief moment, then falls asleep.

"I see the adoration is mutual," I hear Grace say from behind me. I look over and smile.

"She is sweet," I say. "Where's Jason?"

"He wanted to go do some archery with my brother. My dad promised to show him."

"Is that safe?" I wonder out loud, making Grace laugh.

"My dad will help him. Do you want to ride?" she asks.

"I'm not very good, remember?" The only time I ever ride is when I visit my cousins.

"I can put you on Honey Bear, our gentle mare," she assures me.

"Okay. If you think Honey Bear can do all the work," I agree.

"You play with the kittens a little longer, I'll tack up," she says.

She stands up and leaves the loft. I notice the other kittens have worn themselves out and are cuddling together to stay warm as they take a nap. My mind wanders again as I pet the tiny animal in my lap. It is relaxing to be here; maybe I shouldn't go home early. No, I really want my floor routine. I need to be able to do routines in practice like everyone else. I hope Melony makes up something good. Maybe we should have asked Madame Julia to make up my routine. After all the music *is* from a ballet. Then again, she might put things in there that I can't do.

"You ready birthday girl?" I hear Grace call up. "Set the kitten down and let's go!"

Reluctantly, I pick up Snow Queen and set her down on a little bed of hay. She meows at me to let me know she is not happy to be disturbed.

New Challenges

"Sorry little one. I'll be back," I say and stand up.

I climb down the ladder from the loft to the main part of the barn. When I get down Grace is waiting for me and without a word I follow her to the other end of the barn where two horses are waiting bridled and saddled. She unclips the reins where Honey Bear is waiting and hands them to me.

"This is Honey Bear. Just hold these and walk with her. You can follow us," she says as she goes over and unclips her white and gray mare.

"What's her name?" I ask, as she begins to walk with her horse next to her.

"Marshmallow," Grace answers. Honey Bear patiently waits and when it's our turn she starts to walk. I think she's walking me out of the tack room, not the other way around.

I watch the white horse in front of me and smile, Marshmallow is a funny name. I look at Honey Bear, she does have a beautiful light brown coat, but not really the color of honey. We follow Grace out into the yard and she walks us over to a tree stump. Honey Bear knows where she's going and she walks over and stands right next to the tree stump.

"You are going to use this stump as a step stool. Stand on here. Now put your left foot in the stirrup, your hand on the saddle, and pull yourself up. You remember, right?" she asks me.

I nod. It has been a while, but I remember. I do as she says and put my foot in the stirrup, my hand on the saddle, and I swing myself up and onto Honey Bear. Grace hands me the reins, which I didn't even realize she was holding.

"Thanks," I say, taking them.

"You remember how to tell her what you want, right?" she asks and I nod yes. Not because I remember that well, but because I have a feeling Honey Bear is in charge. I look down. It's so much higher up than I remember.

Grace easily swings up onto Marshmallow's saddle without using the tree stump. Then she looks at me, "Ready?"

"I think so," I say hesitantly.

"We'll just take a little walk around a few fields, you'll be fine," she reassures me sensing my slight nervousness.

She makes a little click sound to Marshmallow and she starts walking but Honey Bear stays still. Then I remember I have to make the same clicking sound. I awkwardly try making the clicking sound and Honey Bear starts walking, creating an odd rocking sensation. After a few steps I get used to it and click again telling her to speed up. We catch up with Marshmallow and Grace and walk beside them. I glance at Grace; she has a content expression on her face as she looks out at the fields. The wind picks up her hair and waves it behind her. Her name is perfect for her.

We walk along quietly for a while and as I finally get comfortable she says, "Do you want to trot for a bit?"

I remember that trotting is fun so I nod. She says, "Use a little heel with your click," and she is off, leaving Honey Bear and I behind.

"Well, girl, do you want to stretch your legs?" I ask her. She continues to plod along without a comment. I'm worried I might hurt her if I use my heels too much so I lightly tap my heels into her side and click. She walks a little faster, but not much.

"Come on Honey Bear, lets catch them," I say and try

again with a little more force as I click louder. This time she gets the message and we are off. I can feel my hair lifting with the wind and Honey Bear's strength. The air we are running through is cold and sharp. The sky is vivid blue without a cloud in sight. If it weren't for my breath puffing in front of me and my hands turning red, someone watching us might think it's a summer day.

 We trot the length of a field and when Grace turns a corner she slows down. We catch up to her and Honey Bear slows down without me really doing anything.

 "How do you feel?" she asks me. Her cheeks are rosy and her hair is tangled and I know she loves it out here.

 "Wonderful and cold all at the same time," I admit.

 "Oh sorry, I should have gotten you gloves," she apologizes. "We can head back. If we walk it's not as cold."

 We walk along the edge of the field and I can see their farmhouse in the distance. It looks like it came right out of a storybook with the white and blue trim, the two levels, and the porch with rocking chairs. The barn next to it is a classic red with white trim.

 "Do you like growing up here?" I ask her.

 "Of course. I feel cramped when we visit you guys. Even in that big house of yours," she comments.

 "But we have a pool," I tease, referring to the community pool in our neighborhood.

 "We have a lake."

 "We have a mall."

 "We have horses."

 "We have gymnastics!" I cry.

 She laughs, "You got me there. I don't think we have a

gym nearby for miles."

"You don't, my mom and I looked into it last summer to see if I could workout a few days at a local gym. There's nothing."

"Really? I didn't know that. Is it that bad if you miss? Is that why you're going back tomorrow?" she asks.

"It was not a big deal when I took off a week last summer. I can miss days. I just don't like to," I admit. "I'm going back tomorrow because I'm getting my first floor routine."

"Your first? Haven't you been competing for a few years now?" she asks confused.

I explain to her the difference between compulsories and optionals and how this will be the first routine that is uniquely my own. I tell her how the Level 5 season runs right into the Level 6 season and how I am rushed to be ready.

"Sounds stressful," she concludes.

"Maybe, but I love it."

"And I love the horses so it's a good thing my mom is my mom and Heather is your mom," she says, making us both laugh.

"Grace?" I ask.

"Hmm?"

"What's it like to get your period?" I ask.

"Whoa, where'd that come from?" she asks as her horse comes to an abrupt stop. She laughs, "I didn't mean, whoa to you! Sorry Marshmallow," she says, leaning down and rubbing her neck. She clicks Marshmallow back to a walk and catches up to us, since Honey Bear didn't stop her pace.

"You haven't gotten it yet?" she asks me. I shake my head embarrassed. It's my thirteenth birthday and I haven't gotten my period. What's worse is I am relived. "How do you know I've gotten mine?"

"I saw your supplies under the cupboard in the bathroom," I admit. "Sorry, I was looking for soap," I quickly add.

She nods in understanding, thinks for a second and says, "I don't know how to explain it. It's not really a big deal. The pads can feel lumpy. Sometimes your stomach hurts."

"My friends at school said that about the stomach hurting. But how does it hurt?" I ask.

"Like a dull ache. Not sharp. It's weird."

"Weird," I repeat, not at all sure I get it.

"Chloe says she doesn't get cramps at all and that hardly anything happens. That's why she can wear the period underwear."

"Chloe!"

"Yeah, she got hers a few months ago."

"But Chloe is only eleven," I say, still in shock.

She shrugs, "My mom said that's normal for kids today." Then she looks at me, "Hopefully you'll get yours soon so you can get your boobs."

"Boobs?"

"Yeah. Both of us started growing our boobs after we got our periods," she shares.

"I don't want boobs!"

"Why not?"

"I think they might throw me off or get in the way. I don't know, they just seem inconvenient for a gymnast," I explain.

"Just wear a big ol' sports bra. You're related to us. They won't get that big. We are all slender with like size Bs. Getting your actual period will be a bigger problem," she says.

"How so?"

"What will you do? What do gymnasts and dancers do when they get their period? My pads would be way too big and Chloe's period underwear are huge. How would you hide all that?"

"I don't know!" I squeak in panic. Now I really don't want to get my period. Ever.

"Do you have any older girls on your team?"

"Yes," I answer. "For the first time in my gymnastics career there are older girls on my team."

"Ask them," she says.

"I hardly know them."

"You asked me out of the blue," she reminds me.

"You're my cousin. I've known you my entire life and you have to stay friends with me," I counter.

"True. Could you ask your mom?" she wonders.

"I guess," I say, disappointed I didn't get much more out of her than Abigail or Katherine.

Maybe it's time to talk to my mom.

Chapter 15

We get back from our ride and Grace teaches me how to untack and care for the horses. It takes almost as long as the ride, but I can tell Grace doesn't mind the work. Hungry now, we head inside.

The other kids are in the kitchen asking for lunch. Everyone is talking at once, which is common for my family. My uncle is preparing lunch for us and my aunt is baking and telling him he's in the way.

"I'm making your birthday cake with love!" she trills at me. I smile, a little embarrassed at all the attention.

"Are you sure your favorite isn't chocolate cake?" my uncle asks. I shake my head no.

"She loves the butter cakes Justin. You have to wait for your birthday for chocolate," she reminds him.

Uncle Justin shuffles us out on the porch for lunch telling us we need fresh air. Grace and I sit on the swing bundled under blankets. Jason and Chloe are smooshed into a rocking chair and Noah is eating on the steps insisting that he isn't cold.

I take a bite out of my sandwich as I watch the sky darken and the clouds roll in.

"It's a good thing we got our ride in this morning," Grace comments. I agree and pull the blanket tighter around me.

"What'd you guys do this morning?" I ask the others.

"Archery," Noah answers and stands up and starts pacing along the deck. I assume it's because he really is cold. "Jason's pretty good," he adds making my brother beam.

"I'm ready to go in," Chloe says standing up and heading inside. Noah immediately follows her without a word.

I look at Jason all alone on the rocking chair, "Do you want to join us?" I offer.

He shakes his head no and says, "I'm better than Noah at archery."

I doubt that but I say, "Nice. Did you show Dad?"

"Yeah, he was there. He's terrible," he shares twisting his face up making us laugh. "I'm serious!" he yells as if he is mad at us. But one thing is for sure, if Jason has caused the laughing he can't stay mad. He gets too delighted with himself.

"You better teach him how to do it then," Grace says.

He nods, satisfied we believe he is the best. Then he stands up and heads inside.

I look at Grace as we swing, "Should we head in?" I ask her.

"Let's wait just a minute. I smell snow. It's going to come down any second. I love the first snow."

"It's already snowed this year," I remind her.

"I mean the first snow that comes down in a storm before things get whipping around," she explains.

I look out at the calm looking empty and brown fields. The sky is gray and gloomy. We swing quietly for a while and watch as the gray gives way to a white sky and then, just as Grace predicted, snowflakes begin to swirl around. They aren't really falling so much as swirling. It's like they came out of the middle of the sky instead the clouds above.

"Where'd they come from?" I ask.

"It's cool, huh?" she replies.

"I like the farm more and more each year," I comment.

"Why do you think?" she asks.

"I don't know. Middle school is hard I guess. The kittens are nicer to me," I say, making Grace laugh.

"Animals are great. I might like them better than people," she admits.

Just then we hear the screen door slam and we turn and look to see my mom holding two mugs. "I thought you two might like some birthday hot chocolate," she says handing us each a mug.

"Thanks Aunt Heather."

"Thanks Mom," I say, taking the mug. It immediately warms my hands. The whip cream on top is swirled perfectly and it has sprinkles on top.

"Why does she get sprinklings?" Grace says in a teasing voice. She holds out her mug that has the whip cream but is, indeed, without sprinkles.

"She's the birthday girl!" my mom exclaims. Then quickly adds, "Jennifer told me it was a new tradition, is that not right?"

Grace laughs, "It is. I'm just messing with you."

My mom smiles in relief and says, "I'll let you two get back to your teenage talk." She sends me a wink and walks back into the house.

Teenage talk. "I don't feel like a teenager."

"Why not, you are one. As of today."

I give Grace a look. She immediately knows what I am scowling about. "Your period? Who cares? It doesn't define how mature you are. You do," she says, sounding very adult. "My mom didn't get hers until she was fourteen," she continues. "When did your mom get hers?"

"I don't know."

"Have you guys talked about it at all?" she asks.

"Not really," I admit.

"Maybe that's why you're so worried."

Maybe. Or maybe I'm worried I'll get my period at practice, or worse, a meet. I'm worried I won't have the stuff to take care of it. What do gymnasts use anyway? It feels like this big secret that everyone knows and no one knows. Kind of like when we do mass in Latin once a month at school. We all kind of know what's happening but at the same time, we don't know the details.

"I'm worried I'm going to keep growing," I finally share.

"Why?"

"Gymnastics has been getting harder lately. I think it's because I'm getting bigger."

"Didn't you just move up like two levels in a year?" she asks me.

"Yeah."

"Maybe that's why it's hard."

I think about this as I watch the snow swirl around. I take a sip of my hot chocolate and wonder about what Grace just said. Maybe gymnastics is harder because I'm trying to be ready for Level 6 so quickly. Maybe I should have taken the extra year like Marissa chose to. Except I like the flexibility of optionals where I can create routines that play to my strengths. Or rather, avoid my weaknesses.

I watch the snow shift from swirling to coming down in larger flakes. I'm glad my mom and I are heading back tomorrow because I think once I have my routines maybe I'll feel better. I look at Grace, a little sad to leave early.

"Mom said we could watch a movie since it's snowing out," Noah calls, poking his head out of the house.

"It is getting cold out here," Grace says and I nod in agreement. We untangle ourselves from the blankets and stand up. Grace hands me her mug and collects the blankets to take inside.

"Mom says Paige gets to decide the movie since it's her birthday," Noah adds.

I don't really care what we watch, but it will be fun to have final say.

The snow doesn't let up after the movie so we start a puzzle up in the bonus room. The five of us get along shockingly well as we sort all 1,000 pieces and began to make the frame. That's the thing about cousins; you don't

New Challenges

take them for granted as much as siblings. You tend to be nicer to them when you play so there are less fights.

"Hey guys!" Aunt Jennifer yells up to us.

We look up from our puzzle and Chloe yells back, "What?"

"Wash your hands and come down for dinner!" she yells.

We reluctantly stop what we're doing and disperse to the two bathrooms upstairs to wash our hands. As we are walking down I smell my favorite dinner, spaghetti and meatballs. When I get to the dining room there are now balloons to go with the sign, gifts on the table, and a cake.

"Wow, thank you," I say to all the adults, because I know it was a team effort.

"Happy Birthday pumpkin," my mom says coming over to give me a hug.

"Do the presents now!" Jason exclaims.

"Let's have dinner first while it's hot," Aunt Jennifer says, setting a salad on the table.

"Wait," my mom says picking up the salad Aunt Jennifer just set down. "Pictures first."

We take pictures with me and the cake, banner, and cousins and then we are allowed to start dinner. As usual, everyone is talking at once. Grace is reporting on the horses, Jason is talking about wanting to do a magic show, the adults keep talking about remembering their thirteenth birthday, and Chloe and Noah keep arguing about who gets the flower on the cake. I smile to myself, it's a perfect dinner.

When we are done with dinner Uncle Justin dims the lights and everyone starts singing Happy Birthday while

Aunt Jennifer brings me the cake with thirteen candles. As soon as they are done singing I pause to think of a wish. I wish for a successful Level 6 season. Then I take a deep breath and blow out the candles.

My mom takes the cake and starts cutting it and serving pieces to everyone while Aunt Jennifer moves me to the family room to open gifts. Uncle Justin and Noah stay in the kitchen to clean the dishes. They make it clear I can't open their gift until they are done. I sit down in the family room and there are three packages sitting on the coffee table in festive birthday wrap with red, yellow, and green balloons.

The first one is a pair of stud earrings with my birthstone from my parents.

"Every teenage girl needs a nice pair of earrings," my mom says.

"Thanks Mom," I say and put the earrings on. The second gift is a book and a deck of cards from Jason and the third gift is a beautiful red and white workout leotard from my parents.

"We're so proud of how hard you've worked. A new leotard seemed appropriate," my mom says with pride.

"Thanks Mom," I say again, reaching over to hug her.

"Ready for our gift?" Chloe squeals with excitement. I look at the coffee table and there are no packages on the table. I look at her confused.

"Grace is getting your present," Aunt Jennifer says.

"Hold on! We want to see this!" Uncle Justin says as he and Noah come in from the kitchen to watch me get my present.

"Ready?" we hear Grace yell from outside and Aunt

New Challenges

Jennifer yells back that we are ready.

As Grace walks in the door with a brown box everyone is very quiet, which for this group, is rare. Grace slowly walks across the room and hands me the box. When she puts it in my lap I can feel it moving. It can't be.

I lift the lid and there is Snow Queen meowing away with a green bow around her neck. She sees I have lifted the lid and pops her head up with a loud indignant cry making the group laugh.

"Really?!" I exclaim, lifting her out of the box.

"Grace said you two hit it off," Aunt Jennifer beams at us.

"Mom?" I ask, in shock that I can really have a kitten.

"I think you are responsible enough to handle her," my mom says with a huge grin.

I snuggle her to my cheek and try not to cry. This is the best birthday ever!

Chapter 16

The next day the snow is coming down so we don't ride. We do visit the animals since they still need to be fed. I, of course, opt to go to the loft to check on Mama and the rest of the kittens. I kept Snow Queen with me in the bonus room last night. She cried and cried until she wore herself out and fell asleep at my feet.

Now she is tucked under my arm as I climb up the ladder. "Why don't you hang out here today with your mom and siblings. I'll come get you before we leave this afternoon." I set her down and she slowly walks to her siblings. They seem not to have noticed her absence. "You knew. Isn't that right Mama?" I ask the mama cat. She

New Challenges

looks at me warily. "I'll take good care of her," I promise.

I sit down and start scooping the food in a bowl. At the sound of my scraping all the kittens come running. "I'm going to miss you guys."

Once they are done eating, I play with them while I listen to Jason, Chloe, and Grace talk to the horses below. The horses are cool, but somehow I feel more at ease with the kittens. I'm a little bit sad to leave this afternoon, but I'm excited to go home and learn my new floor routine. Plus, I need to get back home to work on homework, too. There are a few projects due before Christmas that I have put off. I wonder how long they will really take.

"Paige?" I hear Grace yell up to me interrupting my thoughts.

"Yeah?" I yell down.

"We are done here; do you want to go back in with us?" she asks.

"Yeah, just a sec," I answer, standing up. "Mama, kittens," I acknowledge them. "Snow Queen, I will be back for you this afternoon." She is busy trying to bite off her green ribbon and doesn't respond. I take pity on her and reach down and untie it. "There you go. See you later."

I climb back down the ladder. My cousins and brother are waiting for me at the bottom. Without a word we tighten our coats and walk back to the house together.

"Can we go sledding?" Jason asks.

"There aren't any hills, silly," Chloe says.

"Oh yeah," Jason says, sounding deflated. "I'm used to our neighborhood," he comments.

"The mountains are a little farther for us," Grace comments. "You're right though, this would be perfect sledding snow," she says trying to make him feel better.

"We can still make snow angels," I say running and jumping onto a fluffy section of snow sitting over the grass in the yard. The others follow me and pretty soon the front yard is full of snow angel imprints and we have snow down our backs.

Noah hears the ruckus and, not wanting to miss the fun, comes out and joins us. I look up at the gray sky with snow coming down, I take in a cold crisp breath, and move my arms and legs to create a new angel. When my neck can't take the cold any longer I sit up. My angel mark looks pretty good. I look over at Chloe, "The trick is getting up without ruining it," she says, also sitting up.

We both carefully stand up and step out of our angel imprint without ruining it with footprints. "Mom, look!" Chloe yells to her mom who has come out onto the porch to see what all the commotion is about.

"'Tis the season," Aunt Jennifer says.

Noah bounces up, "Can we go get a tree now?"

"The snow is too bad today. We'll go up tomorrow," she comments.

I realize I'm going to miss the fun of picking out a tree tomorrow and probably decorating it. I wish I could be two places at once. Or, if I'm wishing, I just wish their farm was closer to us. Or maybe that a gym was out here. Then we could just move here. Although, I don't think my parents care much for the farm, even though my mom was raised on one.

"I'm sad I'm going to miss getting the tree," I comment.

"Then stay!" Chloe squeals.

New Challenges

"We'd love to have you and your mom stay one more day," Aunt Jennifer adds.

I shake my head. They don't get it. I don't say any more about it in fear that Aunt Jennifer talks my mom into staying.

We spend the day playing games and working on the giant puzzle. The afternoon arrives quickly and before I know it my mom tells me to go pack up to go home. I reluctantly pull myself away from the puzzle I am working on with my cousins. I wonder if going back a day early is worth it as I stuff my clothes in my bag and roll up my sleeping bag.

I hear the other kids talking about what movie they want to watch tonight.

"We could watch a Christmas one. Thanksgiving is over and we're decorating tomorrow," Chloe reasons.

I sigh and stand up, grabbing my pillow and bag. I sling my bag over my shoulder and walk over to my cousins and brother.

"You're leaving already?" Grace asks. I nod and she gives me a hug. Chloe and Noah do the same. Jason just gives me a fist bump. He's decided lately that he's too old for hugs.

"Bye, Jay," I say and grab a hug anyway. He wiggles out of it but doesn't complain.

"Don't have too much fun without me," I say even though I know they will.

I head down the stairs and they go back to their puzzle. I walk outside and find my mom and dad packing the car. I hand my mom my bag and she puts it in the trunk.

"Ready pumpkin?" She asks.

"Hold on," I hear Aunt Jennifer say, as she walks down the stairs with a cat carrier in her hand. "Let's go get your little girl," she says to me.

I happily grab the carrier and head to the barn with my aunt to get Snow Queen. "I was hoping she would forget," I hear my dad grumble under his breath.

As I walk across the yard I worry about Mama as I take one of her babies away. I stop and turn to my aunt, "I don't think I can do it."

"What?" my aunt asks, surprised.

"I can't take her from Mama," I explain.

My aunt laughs and walks over to me, takes the cat carrier, and says, "You city kids. She'll be fine. They will be going off on their own soon anyway." She strides toward the barn. I stand rooted to my spot.

"I can't do it," I say. All I can see is Mama cat watching me take her baby.

Aunt Jennifer stops and turns back to look at me. "I'll do it. She'll understand, I promise." She doesn't try to talk me into coming with her, she just walks to the barn with the carrier swinging at her side. I watch her disappear into the barn and although I am curious to see how Mama takes it, I can't move. I stand and wait for what feels like forever. Hopefully Aunt Jennifer is explaining to Mama that Snow Queen is going to a good home.

Finally, my aunt emerges from the barn with a loudly meowing Snow Queen in the cat carrier. She walks up to me and hands me the carrier.

"She's crying because of the carrier. I know she's happy to go with you. Grace told me about how you two bonded." I tentatively take the carrier, still feeling bad about Mama. "Trust me, her life will be better with you. Some of them won't make it through the winter."

"Then why don't you bring them in?" I ask.

"As much as we would love to, it would just be too many animals inside. Farm life is different, Paige," she explains.

I nod as if I understand, but I don't. I walk to the car and I see my mom is waiting by the car to hug her sister goodbye. I climb into the front passenger seat. I settle Snow Queen in my lap and quietly tell her everything is going to be okay. I don't think she believes me though because she won't stop yowling.

Chapter 17

We made it home from the farm with plenty of time to have a relaxing evening. We had to stop at the pet store on the way home to get Snow Queen kitty litter, cat food, bowls, and a few toys. Once home, I let her explore the house. Mom and I decided to put her box in the laundry room and her food in the kitchen. I sat with her in the laundry room until she discovered her box. Then I scooped her up and took her to my room. She meowed and meowed probably feeling so out of place without her mom and siblings. Eventually, she wore herself out and fell asleep on my bed. It didn't take me long to join her and fall asleep, too.

New Challenges

It's now Sunday morning and I'm getting ready to go to practice and I hate to leave her. "I'll be back in a couple of hours. I think we are going to have to lock you in the laundry room so you don't get lost," I try to explain to her.

She's not listening as she sniffs my dirty clothes basket. I put on the new leo I got for my birthday. Now that we're home I'm so excited to go to the gym and get my routine. I dig through my drawer of leos, shorts, and leggings. I decide to put on leggings. It's Sunday; no classes will be going on so the gym will probably have the heat on low.

Then I put my hair in a single fluffy ponytail, throw a sweatshirt on, pull on my fuzzy boots and I'm ready. I scoop up Snow Queen and carry her down the hall to the laundry room. I set her down and she immediately makes a run for the door. I have to pick her up again, place her in the middle of the room, and quickly shut the door. I can hear her meowing behind the door, making me feel terrible.

"I'll be back soon!" I yell through the door to her.

I run down the stairs and I find my mom quietly having a cup of coffee and doodling designs in her notebook.

"Morning mom," I say, making her look up.

"Good morning pumpkin," she greets. "Are you ready for this?"

"So ready," I say, grabbing a banana.

"Do you want anything else?" she asks me. I think about how I'm growing so much, maybe I shouldn't have more than a banana. Then my stomach growls.

"Yeah, maybe some toast or something." As much as I want to be small, I don't know how anyone ignores their stomach.

"You may have to eat this in the car," she says, putting a piece of bread in the toaster. I look at the clock and agree.

"How is Snow this morning?" she asks me.

"You mean Snow Queen?" I ask.

"I thought I would call her Snow for short," she says, I frown thinking about that nick name. I'm not sure.

"She's not happy about being in the laundry room. But I think if I leave her to roam the house I won't find her when I get back."

"She's pretty tiny and could get lost. I think you're right," she says, pulling out my toast, putting butter on it, and handing it to me wrapped in a napkin.

"Thanks," I say, taking it appreciatively.

"Shall we?" she asks.

I nod, "Are you staying?" I ask, with my mouth full of toast.

"I thought I would. I have my book."

"It will be more exciting than your book," I tease her as we walk to the garage.

We get there a few minutes before Melony and the gym is locked. We are the only ones in the parking lot. My mom and I are quiet for a moment. Maybe I should ask her what I'm supposed to do about wearing a leotard when I get my period.

I remain silent, trying to get up the courage to talk to her when I see Melony pull up. My mom probably wouldn't know the answer anyway. I mean, she wasn't a gymnast. Then again, she is a mom.

Without a word, my opportunity is over as we both step out of the car.

Melony greets us as we hustle to the door. The sun is

out, but the air is cold and snow is on the ground. As we are entering the gym I see a couple more cars pull up.

"Who else is coming?" I ask.

"Oh, I invited Savannah and Lucy to work on their routines this morning too. All of you just haven't had as much time with your routines," she says.

Since we have the gym to ourselves, I don't bother going upstairs to the optionals room. I pull off my boots and toss them in a cubby in the lobby. Lucy and Savannah walk in with their moms behind them.

"Good morning," I say.

"This is going to be fun," Debbie says, super bubbly for first thing in the morning. "Let's grab a chair from the coaches room so all three of us can sit in the training area," she says disappearing into the training offices.

"Come on in girls," Melony says. "It's a bit cold, but I just turned up the heaters. Why don't you run a little and we'll get started."

Lucy, Rose, Savannah, and I start running. As soon as we round the first corner Savannah asks me, "How was the farm?"

"Awesome! I got a kitten!"

"You did?" Lucy exclaims.

"Yeah, for my birthday," I explain.

"It's your birthday?" Lucy asks.

"Yesterday."

"How old are you?" she asks.

"Thirteen."

"Wow," she huffs as she runs. "How does that feel?"

"I don't know. The same I guess."

"What does she look like?" Savannah asks.

"Who?" I ask, getting lost in all the questions they are firing at me.

"The kitten!" Savannah exclaims. "I can't believe I haven't talked my mom into a kitten," she marvels.

"Oh, she's so cute! She is all white with black ears and face, and blue eyes."

"What's her name?" Lucy asks.

"Snow Queen."

"I can't wait to meet her," Savannah says.

"We should have brought her," I say, regretting leaving her in the laundry room.

We slow down on our last lap and stop in the middle of the floor. Since this isn't an official workout we skip our jumps and sit down in our splits to stretch.

"How was your Thanksgiving?" I ask my teammates.

Savannah shrugs, "Quiet. Just my mom and my grandma. I think my mom was bummed you didn't stay. She likes people. On Friday we had a friendsgiving. A bunch of her friends from college and work came over, so that was nice for her. Honestly, I liked the quiet day better."

I nod, understanding Savannah. She likes to be social, but it seems like she likes small groups better.

I turn to Rose, who has been quiet all this time, "What are you working today?"

"I think I have to stay on floor with you because James can't come in today. So probably my round-off back handspring, back handspring. I need to clean up my form on the second one."

"Are you guys ready?" Melony asks, walking up to us. We nod and she starts to give instructions. "Lucy and Savannah, ten of each of the dance skills in your routine in front of the mirrors while I work with Paige. When you are done, I'll watch a dance through and tell you what you need to work on after that." Then she turns to Rose, "Rose, since you are off season I want you work on getting your steps into the pit."

"How do I do that?" Rose asks.

"Start on the edge of the floor in front of the pit and do your round-off back handspring from there. See how far it is and then try doing a round-off back handspring punch into the pit."

Rose lights up at this idea and runs over to the edge of the floor by the pit. Lucy and Savannah walk over to the mirror and begin working their dance skills.

Melony looks at me and smiles, "Ready?"

I smile back, "Ready."

"I have had so much fun creating this routine for you. Some parts might be challenging, but if you don't get it, we can change it."

"I'll get it," I say, confident in my ability to dance.

"I think so too," she says walking over to the gym stereo at the edge of the floor. She plugs in the gym phone and scrolls down to where it says, *Paige's music – Swan Lake*. She looks at me and says, "Let's listen to the first few eight counts so you have the rhythm in your head before I teach you the first section." She turns on the music and I remember how much I love it. "Listen to how it starts slow and flowy," she says.

We are quiet for a minute while we listen. Then she starts it over and counts over the music so I can hear the counts. I nod and she starts it again and says, "You're going to be still for the first eight and come in on the one of the second eight count."

"Okay," I say with confidence. I can hear the counts well and I know what she means.

"Let me teach you the first sixteen counts then," she turns off the music and walks a few feet away and I follow her.

"I want you to start here facing the corner," she says and shows me my starting pose, which is very beautiful with my arms in fourth position and my back toe pointed behind me with my legs straight. She has me do some flowy arm movements before I slowly move to the corner.

I learn the sixteen counts quickly and I love what she has put together so far. It's very balletic in its movement, which is what I wanted.

"Practice that first part into the corner while I have these two do dance throughs for me," she instructs.

I do as she says and practice my new dance section from the beginning to where I get myself to the corner ready to tumble. I am dying to try it to the music but Lucy is playing her music right now.

As soon as she and Savannah are done, I ask, "Can I try it to the music?"

"Five times at least," Melony says and walks over to check on Rose's progress.

Lucy hears this and asks, "Want me to turn it on for you?" as she walks over to the stereo.

"Yes please," I say getting into my starting pose.

"I like it already," she says as she presses play.

I do my sixteen counts, but not quite right and without a word I start again and Lucy starts the music over. We do this several times until Melony comes back.

"Thanks Lucy, I'll take it from here so you can go work leaps," she says, taking the phone from her. Lucy nods and gets back to work. Melony looks at me, "Let me see it to the music and we'll move on."

I show her the sixteen counts to the music and this time I get it. The moms clap and cheer from their chairs just inside the training area. I grin and do a pretend curtsy, making them clap louder.

Melony just says, "Over here," and she walks to the other end of the floor to where I would end my first tumbling pass. Then she shows me a few poses into my leap pass. Then a few more poses and I am to my second and final tumbling pass.

"That was fast," I say.

"I put a lot of dance at the end so that will be what judges remember," she wisely says.

"Good call," I say, knowing that my dance ability far exceeds my tumbling skills.

"Let's learn to the end of your second pass today," she decides.

"I can learn all of it," I plead.

"Probably, but I find it ends up cleaner if you learn a little at a time. Besides knowing through the second pass is enough to do it in practice and get your floor conditioning up."

I agree, but I'm bummed. I thought I would leave today knowing my entire routine. The Level 6 and 7 routines are so short I shouldn't have to split it up.

"Besides, I'm not entirely sure about a few of the dance moves until I see how the first half looks on you," she explains.

"Okay," I say so morosely that she starts laughing.

"Paige, you have most of your routine. Don't be disappointed. You have something to work on in practice now. That was worth coming in for," she reminds me.

She's right; it was. I do my partial routine to the music several times. It surprises me how it does wear me out more than the Level 5 routine ever did. The movements are harder and after the first tumbling pass the energy level is higher and faster.

"That's enough for today Paige," Melony finally says to me. Then to the group, "Girls, stretch it out and then you can go!"

We happily sit in a circle stretching. Since this is a voluntary workout we don't have conditioning nor is Melony telling us what to stretch. She is over talking to the moms.

"Your routine is beautiful," Lucy says as we sit down.

"Thanks," I say with a grin.

"Do you like it?" Savannah asks.

"So far," I say, "But I'm sad I didn't learn the entire thing." I admit.

We are silent for a brief moment before Rose says, "I can't wait to be in optionals." This makes me smile. I remember that feeling so well; being stuck with the monotonous compulsory routines. With that one statement Rose made me grateful to have even half of a routine. Because it's *my* half; no one else's.

Chapter 18

That afternoon I practice the first half of my routine over and over in my room. When the sun goes down my mom pokes her head in.

"Why don't you come down for dinner pumpkin," she invites me. I stop what I'm doing and think for a moment. Now that she mentions it, I am hungry. I look at Snow Queen curled up on my bed.

"Okay," I say, "But what if she wakes up? She still doesn't know the house very well."

"Bring her down. She can explore the kitchen."

I look at my white ball-of-fur kitten and I hate to wake her; but I hate the idea of leaving her more. I scoop her up and carry her down to the kitchen. She wakes and meows at me and it feels like she is saying, 'Now where are you taking me?'

I set her on the family room couch which is just off the kitchen. She immediately walks back and forth on the couch and cries.

"Let her be, she's just getting used to the house," my mom says, pulling containers of Thanksgiving leftovers out of the fridge that we brought back from the farm. "Here, make a plate of your favorites," she instructs.

I walk up to the counter and take one of the plates she set out and I fill it with mashed potatoes, stuffing, and corn. I go to put my plate in the microwave and my mom plops a piece of turkey on my plate.

"You need protein to grow," she justifies.

I don't say anything, but continue to the microwave asking, "How long?"

"Start with 45 seconds and then let's take a look."

I set the microwave and watch my plate through the window going in circles.

"What if I don't want to grow anymore?" I ask her.

"What?" my mom asks confused as she piles her plate with something from every container.

"You said the protein will make me grow. What if I don't want to grow anymore?" I repeat.

She stops mid scoop and looks at me, "Why wouldn't you want to grow?" she asks perplexed.

"Because I'm a gymnast. And I'm tired of being the tallest on the team and of people telling me how tall I am."

"Oh pumpkin, I had no idea that bothered you," she apologetically replies. I shrug and keep watching my food.

"First of all I hardly think five feet is tall."

My food beeps and I look at her, "But everyone keeps telling me how tall I'm getting."

"That's because you grew a lot in a short amount of time. That doesn't mean you're a tall human being. Look, Paige, you aren't going to be a gymnast forever and you are going to want a little more height."

I'm not so sure about that, I think, as I reach up and take my food out. I walk it over to the counter and sit down while she heats up her food. I poke at the meat on my plate. If the protein represents growth, then I don't want to eat it.

"What's wrong with a tall gymnast anyway?" she asks.

"Nothing, I guess. It's just hard," I admit.

"What's hard?" she asks.

"Everything. Mostly floor. Tumbling has gotten really hard for me. Skills I already have feel like I'm just learning them. They're awkward and clunky."

"I had no idea. You had such a great workout today," she points out.

"That's because I was just doing dance today."

My mom frowns as she brings her plate around and sits next to me. Then she turns to me with a very serious expression.

"Paige, growing is part of life. I'm sorry it's making gymnastics difficult, but in the big picture of your life, you want to be the height you were meant to be. You don't want to cut out food or dislike your body because it's not the norm for gymnasts."

I look down and stab my rubbery microwaved turkey again. She sees me do it and says, "Plus, protein is energy and strength, too. You need energy to be able to do gymnastics in the first place."

"Can't I just stop growing for now?" I whine.

This is where Jason would have laughed or made a joke. Since he's still at the farm the mood remains solemn and my mom is intently looking at me.

"I'm sad you feel this way pumpkin. You need to stay healthy and let nature help you grow to the size you were meant to be."

"Am I going to get my period soon?" I ask, surprising both of us.

"I imagine so. I guess I've been so wrapped up in my own stuff I haven't talked to you about it."

"It's okay," I say. "Grace and Chloe both got theirs. I talked to them. Well, to Grace."

"I see," my mom says, sounding a little hurt. "Chloe, too?"

"I thought that was crazy, too!" I exclaim.

"Girls are getting it younger these days," she comments.

She takes a bite and finally says, "Do you have any questions for me? Or did Grace answer them all for you?"

"What do I do when I get it? I mean, about gymnastics?"

"I imagine you will have to learn to use a tampon."

"What's that?" I ask.

"I'll get you some at the store tomorrow and you can see. But basically, you put it inside your body and it absorbs the bleeding so you can do sports or swim and forget you are having your period at all."

"So, it like, goes inside?"

"Yes."

"Gross."

"It's not gross; it's your body. Your body does so many amazing things, this is just one more. Your body is preparing to create babies if you want them. Don't you think that's kind of cool? Your body can create a human!"

I pause and think about what she said. It is kind of amazing when she says it like that. But babies seem so far away, why does my body have to get ready now?

"Does it hurt?" I ask.

"It can. It's more uncomfortable," she says.

I sigh, "I don't want to get it," I decide.

My mom laughs, "You can't stop it pumpkin. It's just one of those facts of life."

She is quiet for a moment. I decide to follow her lead and eat in silence. It's not hard to be quiet. We're so used to Jason talking all the time that when he's gone we struggle to make dinner conversation.

"When do you think they'll get back?" I ask. I thought my dad and Jason would be back from the farm by now.

"Dad said not until late. I guess they had a fun morning cutting down a Christmas tree."

"Lucky," I sigh. "Can we watch a movie?"

"Yes. Actually, I have an idea of what we should watch," she says with a grin.

"What?" I say.

"It's a surprise. You clean up here, I'm going to see if I can find what I want to watch," she says, getting up from the counter and going into the family room to pull up movies on the TV.

I look at the mess out on the counter, it looks bad but shouldn't take too long to clean. I rinse off our plates and put them in the dishwasher. Then I put away the food containers in the fridge. When I'm done with the kitchen I text Katherine and Abigail that we are back from Thanksgiving. I think of Snow Queen and text them that I have a surprise to tell them at school tomorrow.

Katherine:
    Did you get a boyfriend?
Abigail:
    Did you get your period?

I laugh, they both seem equally unlikely.

Me:
    I'll tell you tomorrow.

Based on the questions they fired back at me, they might be disappointed by the announcement of Snow Queen.

"Are you ready for a great movie?" my mom sounds happy with whatever we are going to watch. We settle into the family room and my mom already has a streaming app up on the TV.

"What are we watching?" I ask.

"Freaky Friday," she says, pulling a blanket up over us.

Chapter 19

I get to our lunch table before Katherine or Abigail. I sit down and pull out my lunch and my phone and start to scroll through my pictures. I decide on one from my birthday where she is still wearing the green bow.

"What's the big news?" Katherine asks walking up.

I extend my arm out and turn my phone to her so she can see the picture of Snow Queen.

"Oh my gosh, she is darling! Is that the news? Is she yours?"

I nod, "Her name is Snow Queen."

"What is it? I want to see!" Abigail demands walking up to our table. I show the picture to her.

"Why are we looking at this kitten?" she asks.

"It's Paige's new kitten!" Katherine exclaims.

"Really? She's your news?"

"She is," I say turning the phone back to me to look for another picture. I scroll through and land on one from last night when we were watching the movie.

"A kitten *is* big news," Abigail decides. "You'll have her forever."

"I hope so," I say as I hold out another picture. They are less interested this time so I put my phone down and pull out my sandwich.

"How were your Thanksgivings?" I ask. They both tell me about their weekends. Abigail visited her grandma's house in Oregon and she told us about how they shopped and went to the movies. Katherine went to Park City with her family for a ski trip. "The snow was just okay this early in the season. The hot tub at the house was amazing though," she shares.

"How was the farm?" Abigail asks.

"Awesome! That's where I got Snow Queen."

"Who's Snow Queen?" Abigail asks.

"The kitten. Keep up."

"The kitten. My kitten," I confirm. "There was an entire litter in the loft. They were so cute. I wish I could have taken all of them home."

I tell them more about the farm; the mama cat, her kittens, and horseback riding. I even tell them about the snowstorm and the giant puzzle.

"Your weekend sounds better," Abigail decides.

"Maybe I can bring you guys out to the farm sometime," I say. Grace would love these two. I'm not sure what Chloe would think and Noah would probably be annoyed. Maybe not. "Or maybe I could bring Grace out here and you guys could meet her," I amend.

"When do we get to see this kitten?" Katherine asks.

"Yeah! Let's come over today!" Abigail decides.

"I have practice today," I remind them.

"Oh yeah," she says, her face falling.

"I don't tomorrow though," I quickly add.

"Ask your mom if we can go home with you tomorrow," Katherine tells me. I nod just as the bell rings for us to go back to class.

As I'm walking back I wonder what it must be like to be Katherine and Abigail. They get to do whatever they please every day after school.

That afternoon, as I'm getting ready to go to the gym, I talk to Snow Queen about where I'm going and how long I'll be. I make sure to remember my phone because it has my floor music on it . . . and pictures of Snow Queen.

Practice starts on beam. The beam assignment is five stuck routines. As usual, Katie calls me over to give me my separate assignment.

"You are pretty set on beam Paige; you just need beam dance and a series or a flight element. How is the handstand back extension roll combination going?"

"It's hard, but I can do them sometimes on low beam,"

I share.

She nods and says, "Keep doing them there. If you have to stop between the two skills in the intersquad, you have to stop."

"What happens if I stop?"

"You get a deduction for not having a requirement," she explains. "I want you to attempt the series ten times on the low beam and five on high beam with the stop. Then five of everything in your routine and you can spend any remaining time on round-offs."

"Okay," I agree. It's a big assignment that will definitely keep me busy while everyone else is doing routines.

I decide to start with the version on high beam where I step down and can stop if I need to. I can do a handstand and I can do a back extension roll. Doing them connected can't be that hard. *Except it is hard* a little voice says in my head. I shake my head to get that thought out and lift my arms for my handstand. I kick up to a nice tight handstand and step down into a lunge. A lunge does me no good. I can't connect anything with my feet apart like this. I sigh and try again. I kick up to a handstand, step down one foot and then the other one, staggered but right next to the first foot. I stand all the way up, pause for a second, and squat down into my back extension roll. I am crooked and step down off to the side of the beam. I am smiling because I think I can do this, I almost connected it.

"Keep your arms moving the entire time!" I hear Katie yell at me from a few beams away.

I nod, I know I paused. I step up again. This time I pause a little less, but I'm off to the side. The following time I pause longer and almost make my back extension roll. Adding a handstand is harder than it seems.

By the time Katie comes over my head is starting to hurt from so many back extension rolls. She silently watches a few. I do my three best ones (still a pause, still off to the side) while she is watching.

"I think you can get that. What do you think?" she asks me.

"By when?" I ask.

"Christmas."

"I can get it," I say with more confidence than I'm feeling.

She nods and says, "I saw you rubbing your head. Go on to five of everything in your routine and if you still have time then round-offs."

Even though I don't have a routine, per se, I know what will be in it. I have to have a full turn, a leap pass, mount, dismount, a series, and a jump combination.

"What's my mount?" I ask Katie, realizing I don't have one to work.

"Melony will decide when she creates your dance. Speaking of dance, how did the floor routine go?" she asks.

"It's awesome, the dance is really pretty."

"I'm sure it is. I imagine Melony will use a lot of the dance from your floor routine for beam. You can learn it this weekend."

I make a note in my head that I will probably have to come in extra this weekend. I don't mind. Aside from leaving poor Snow Queen, I don't mind.

"A beam is open," Katie says to Maya as Lucy jumps down and heads over to the low beams.

New Challenges

"Done with your five, Lucy?" Katie asks. She and Lucy start talking about what extra skills Lucy can work. I jump up on a beam to work my leaps, turns, and jumps. My back extension roll series is cool, but it's hard. Can I get that by Christmas?

How are Savannah and Lucy so far ahead of me in their preparedness for Level 6? *Because they are better than you* my voice says. When did my voice get so mean? My voice used to be so nice and encouraging.

"Paige, focus!" I hear Katie say to me. How does she know? I miss James. As much as I'm getting used to Katie, I miss James.

"Eyes on the end of the beam!" she yells at me. *Focus. Focus*, I can do that. I fix my eyes on the end of the beam and focus on my split jump, split jump.

"Beautiful! Do it like that every time!" she yells. I give her a tiny nod of acknowledgement and go again. I know it's another good one and I hear Katie give a few claps and walk to the next beam. Thank goodness for dance elements. They save me every time.

"Paige you have got to pull your toes to make it around," James tells me. We are on the last rotation of the day. James is working with us because he is done with the Level 3 practice. Katie is working with the Level 8s, 9s, and 10s on beam. I was so excited to have James coaching us, unfortunately my floor rotation is not going as planned. We don't have access to the entire floor yet. Two classes are using half of the floor and we are tumbling on the other half. James told us we would run routines at the end of the rotation. I'm excited to show my teammates the first half of my routine. That's the only thing keeping me going in this miserable workout.

"What are your passes?" James asks me.

"Layout and front, front," I answer.

"And your first meet is in a month?" he asks.

"About. We have our final intrasquad before Christmas break and our first meet is the first weekend in January."

"What is your back up plan?" he asks me.

"I don't know." *A back up plan? Back up to what?*

"I'll talk to Katie," he says.

"About what?"

"You need a plan B if this layout doesn't become more consistent."

"You think I can't do it?" I ask, feeling my eyes prickle hot. James has always believed in me. I have never had him question if I could make a skill. There are skills he knows would be physically impossible for me, like a back walkover on beam. That was different, he believed I could do the back extension roll instead.

"Paige, you are a very talented athlete and you work hard. I believe you can get these skills. By moving up form Level 5 to 6 in the same year, you gave yourself very little time to prepare. A back up plan might be a good idea."

I lift my chin, "Then why hasn't Katie mentioned it?" I ask defiantly.

"Because Katie has five optionals teams she's trying to

keep track of," he fires back at me.

"She lost track of me?" I say, trying even harder to keep my watery eyes from giving me away.

"Not exactly, I bet she's just waiting to see what you do at the intrasquad. I think it would be a good idea for you to have an A and B routine on floor."

"A and B?" I ask. Out of the corner of my eye I see Maya motion for James to spot. He nods and motions for me to move off to the side of the floor and waves for her to go. He spots her, gives a correction, and turns back to me.

"Work both layouts and tucks today. Then work both bounders and single front tucks," he instructs.

I nod. Ironically, that's what I'm already doing. I do several back tucks when I warm up for layouts and I'm not even doing bounders. I'm doing front tuck, stop, front tuck into the pit. The gut punch is hearing that James thinks I need a back-up plan.

I slowly walk back to my place in line to tumble back up the floor to the other end. I run and do a lame punch front. I land in a deep squat, which is uncharacteristic of me. What is wrong with me? Why is my tumbling so low? My front tucks used to land so light and airy and never in a deep almost bum hitting squat.

"Flip on the way up Paige!" James yells to me. I nod as I walk back in line, but I don't turn to look at him, I can feel my face burning in embarrassment. When did I become bad at floor? When is this rotation going to be over? And here I was excited to do floor today. I fumbled through an entire work out only to be miserable at my favorite event.

I just want to go home and see Snow Queen, or hang out with Katherine and Abigail, or workout with my old

Level 5s. I wonder what Trista and Carmen are doing tonight.

After another several miserable tumbling passes the recreational kids finish their rotation on floor and we get the entire floor for the last fifteen minutes of practice. Normally we would be conditioning by now but James decides we will do floor dance throughs as conditioning.

"Ladies, one dance through each with three sprints per tumbling pass. Push-ups and V-ups along the edge of the floor while you wait for your turn. Three sets of ten and then stretch."

It's an easy assignment as far as conditioning goes and we're all smart enough not to say anything and to just get to work.

I'm not sure if I'm supposed to do my half routine or not. I quietly do my push-ups as I watch my teammates huff through dance throughs. James pauses the music when they get to a tumbling pass and they sprint along the diagonal three times rather than doing a tumbling pass. When I get to V-ups everyone has gone except for me.

"Paige, didn't you learn your routine this weekend?" James asks me.

"Half of it."

"Come on up," he motions for me to get up. "Let's do the half you know. Something is better than nothing."

I slowly stand up, nervous and excited to do my routine for my teammates for the first time. I walk to the corner and stand in my starting pose and James starts the music. As soon as my music begins the entire gym stops. All the kids and coaches recognize the new floor music and they want to see a new routine. I do the dance Melony taught me to the corner and when I pause to tumble James pauses the music and I run across the diagonal.

"Great music," I hear Maya saying and it makes me smile a little as I run back the way I came. When I'm done with my three sprints I get in a lunge as if I finished my first tumbling pass and James plays the music. I listen closely to hear when to start dancing again. I do my dance and leap pass and make my way to the next corner. I sprint again, end in a lunge, and then drop my arms and look at James.

"That's it. That's all I know."

He pauses the music, "That's most of it anyway. Great routine Paige. It will be a judge pleaser for sure. Good job today. Go stretch with your teammates."

I don't say anything to him, I just turn and go to where my teammates are sitting along the edge of the floor. I sit down in my splits and my teammates immediately start talking.

"I recognize that music. What's it from?" Victoria asks.

"A ballet," Savannah answers.

"Which one?"

"Swan Lake," I supply.

"It's beautiful. It looks so good on you," Riley says.

"I wish I could dance like that," Alexis comments.

"Thanks," I say, a bit embarrassed by all the praise.

"Paige likes ballet class. That's what it looks like when you pay attention in ballet class," James says walking up and dropping a panel mat in front of us for over splits.

Embarrassed and pleased, I put my foot up on the mat James brought over and slide into over splits.

"I can't wait to see the end," Maya says.

"When do you learn the rest of it?" Savannah asks.

"I'm not sure," I stammer.

"Try for tomorrow," James advises. "I would text Melony and see if she can meet with you before or after the Level 4s and 5s tomorrow."

"Text Melony?" I ask. I've never texted a coach before.

James nods, "Get it done as soon as possible so you can start conditioning for a full set. I'll give your mom her number before you leave." Then he starts talking to Brooklyn about her tumbling passes. In usual James fashion he walks around and adjusts our splits while he chats. I do miss him, even if he doesn't fully believe in me anymore.

Chapter 20

I sit in the car eating a snack as my mom rushes me from school to the gym so I can work with Melony on my floor routine before she coaches the Level 4s and 5s. It's Tuesday, my day off from practice. This won't feel like practice though. Learning dance is easy and fun.

Jason is chattering the entire drive and when my mom pulls up to the gym I jump out without a word.

"How long do you think you'll be?" she asks as I'm getting out.

"Probably only an hour because the Level 4s and 5s start practice in an hour," I answer.

"We'll just go get a snack and come back then," my

mom says. I smile and shut the door, happy to leave Jason's chatter.

I walk into the gym and head straight to the bathroom to change. Then I come out and throw my stuff in a cubby in the lobby, not bothering to go up to the optionals room. The gym isn't busy yet, so the lobby is quiet.

"What are you doing here on a Tuesday?" Suzanne, who works at the front desk, asks me.

"I'm here to finish learning my floor routine."

"I saw that yesterday. It looks great so far. I can't wait to see the rest of it."

"Me either," I say.

"Go on in. Melony is in the office. I'm sure she'll be out soon," she says.

I do as she says and head out into the training area and warm myself up. There is one pre-school class going on and a couple of privates. It's too early for much else, as most kids are still in school.

I'm sitting in my splits when Melony comes out a few minutes later.

"I'm so glad you could come this early. I think we can knock this out today since you learn dance so fast." She sits down in her splits next to me. "There's a lot of dance in the last part."

"I'm ready," I say standing up.

"Great, warm up with a dance through of what you know so far," she instructs.

"With or without music?" I ask.

"Let's do one of each."

I do as she says and do a quiet dance through without the music. Then she turns on the stereo and I do a dance through with the music, which feels so much better.

Melony teaches me the dance after my second tumbling pass. She choreographed pretty and graceful movements that aren't particularly difficult. Then she teaches me a jump combination, shows me where to do my one and a half turn, and teaches me the ending pose.

"That's it?" I say, surprised we're done.

"That's it. Level 6 and 7 floor routines are about half the length of the upper optional routines," she explains.

I knew that. I've been watching the optional girls with envy for years. I just expected it to feel longer once I was the one doing it.

"Plus dance comes easy for you. For some girls it takes a lot more practice to learn and remember their routines. Let's do the second half to music a few more times," she says, walking over to the gym phone. "Start just after the leap pass." I easily do the second half three more times.

"Are you ready for a full dance through?" She asks.

I smile and nod. Of course I'm ready! I can't wait to do the entire thing! I look up to the parent viewing area and I see Jason and my mom are there watching. Well, my mom is watching. Jason is playing video games on his tablet. She sees me look up and waves.

I give her a little wave as I walk to my starting corner. I get in my starting pose and wait for Melony to play the music. I have to concentrate to remember all the dance movements. The music helps me remember what I'm supposed to be doing. I forget a small part after my leap but find the music again for the poses before the tumbling pass.

When I'm done Melony claps as she walks over to me.

"That looked great! Let's just go over the part after the

leap."

I nod while I'm catching my breath. That took more energy than I thought it would. And I didn't even tumble! Imagine how it's going to feel when I put it all together. I keep my concerns to myself as I watch Melony show me the steps again. I repeat them behind her. It helps to do them while she is doing them and I see where I got confused.

"I think I've got it," I say.

"Do it a few more times. Then let's do one more dance through before I have to coach team," Melony instructs.

"It's already time for them to start?" I ask, shocked.

"We've been at it for almost an hour. Time flies when you're having fun," she says over her shoulder as she goes to the stereo to play my music.

I do the segment I struggled with two more times before I feel ready for a final dance through.

As I stand in my corner waiting for the music to begin, I hear the lobby has gotten loud. Classes are starting to come into the training area. The door is swinging open and closed as kids are streaming in.

When my music starts I try to forget the chaos in the lobby and focus on my routine. The music is so powerful and beautiful I have no problem forgetting everything around me and focusing on my dance. I run across the diagonal during my tumbling pass. It crosses my mind to look up at my mom, but I have only eight counts to get to the corner and keep dancing. I get in my lunge and immediately hear the music where I dance again. Then I have my leap pass, more dance, run across the diagonal, one and a half turn, dance, jump, ending pose.

I did it! I have my very own beautiful amazing Swan Lake floor routine!

"That was totally awesome!" I hear someone yell.

I drop my arms from my ending pose and turn to see who it is. Trista is standing there with a huge grin on her face. "I mean it. Totally awesome, Paige."

I'm so happy to see her! "Thanks," I say.

"I'm so glad my mom dropped me off early so I could see that. You should do it one more time so Carmen and Marissa can see it."

I turn to Melony and give her a questioning look.

"Sure, you can do one more while they're running laps around the floor. But then we need to be done. The gym is way too busy this time of day for us to take up the entire floor."

"How have you been?" I ask Trista, as Melony goes back over to the stereo.

"Good. I have my layout on floor. Bars is still the bane of my existence," she says dramatically.

"I miss you guys."

"We miss you, too. Seeing you only one day a week stinks."

"Maybe the summer schedule will be better," I say, hoping it will be true. I really do miss Trista, Carmen, and Marissa.

"Hi Paige. What are you doing here on a Tuesday?" Marissa asks, as she walks into the training room and onto the floor.

"Getting her amazing floor routine," Trista answers.

"Oh, do we get to see it?"

"While you are running laps," I answer.

New Challenges

"How are you?" she asks.

"A little overwhelmed," I answer honestly.

"I bet. I knew it would be too much for me," Marissa says maturely.

"Level 4s and 5s, start running!" Melony yells and then turns to me and yells across the floor, "You ready?"

I nod and walk over to my starting spot, excited and nervous to show my friends my new routine. As I'm standing in my starting pose I see Carmen out of the corner of my eye walk in and it makes me happy that all of my former teammates will see my new routine.

When the music starts, I stop thinking about who is in the gym and force myself to think about the dance. Thankfully the music is so specific and clear, I can remember what goes where.

I do a much better job with the dance before the leap pass, I flub the one and a half turn, and I enjoy the dance at the end. When I'm done my former teammates are clapping as they run their laps around the edge of the floor.

"Great job Paige," Melony says to me. "I want you to go home and do it at least five more times so you don't forget."

"I won't forget," I promise.

"Do it anyway. It's a time-honored tradition to drive your family crazy with your new floor routine," she says. Then she puts her hand on my shoulder, "It's a beautiful routine Paige. I put some difficult dance in there and you learned it with no problem."

"Thanks," I say, a little embarrassed.

"Why don't you stretch with these girls before you leave," she says, gesturing toward the Level 4s and 5s. "I have to talk to Katie before she gets started with the upper optionals."

I happily do as she says and join my friends.

"That was beautiful," Carmen says as soon as I sit in my splits next to her.

"Swan Lake fits you," Marissa adds.

"Thanks guys," I say, surprised I'm a little out of breath.

"The judges are going to love you," Trista says.

"I hope so," I smile. I miss these three. "I miss you guys," I blurt out.

"We miss you, too," Carmen says easily.

"Next season we'll be together. When we are 6s and you are a 7. It will be okay," Trista says. I can tell she has told herself this a lot.

I nod, "You're right. It will be."

"Paige!" I hear my mom loudly whisper to me. I look up and she is looking around the glass training room doors and motioning for me to go.

"I have to go. It was good seeing you guys. Have a good workout," I say, as I stand up and walk to my mom.

As I'm walking out, Melony comes out of the coaches room. "Over and over again tonight, okay?"

"Okay," I agree, knowing that won't be a problem.

"Great job today," she adds.

I feel pleased with myself as I walk out of the training area. I'm going to be able to compete next month after all. I can do this!

"Your routine is gorgeous," my mom says as we walk out of the gym.

"I think so, too," I agree. "I have to practice it tonight

so I don't forget it."

"It's a lot to remember," she comments as we get into the car.

"Can I invite Katherine and Abigail over?"

"I thought you just said you had to practice," my mom says confused.

"I do. I want to show them. They're dancers, they'll get it," I say. "And they are dying to see Snow Queen," I add.

"If you text them right now I can pick them up on the way home."

"Can I have unlimited game time then?" Jason pipes up.

"Why would you get unlimited game time?" my mom asks him.

"Because Paige is getting friends over."

"Jason, that makes no sense. You can have friends over if you want, but no extra games," she tells him.

He slumps back in his seat and keeps playing while he can. He knows when he gets home he has to put it away.

Abigail and Katherine are able to come over. In fact, they were already both hanging out at Katherine's house so we only have to make one stop.

"I thought you didn't have practice on Tuesdays," Katherine says as they get in the car and she sees me in a leo and sweat pants. "I can't keep up," she says squeezing in the back seat. They are in the back with Jason, while I sit up front.

"I cant wait to see your kitten!" Abigail exclaims.

"I don't usually have practice on Tuesdays. I was learning the rest of my floor routine today," I explain.

"Do we get to see it?" Abigail asks.

"I have to go home and do it over and over again, so yes, you get to see it."

"Where will you have room? It's too cold outside for anything," Katherine asks.

"We can push the couches to the walls in the family room," my mom says. "It won't be as big as the real floor, but it should work, right Paige?" she asks me.

"It will work. The dance doesn't have to take up a lot of space. As long as I remember the pattern in my head."

We pull up to the house and the girls are talking over the top of each other arguing over who gets to make up my next floor routine.

"I am going to be a famous choreographer, so it should be me," Abigail says.

"That's fine, because I'm going to be too busy designing clothes," Katherine fires back. While they are arguing I run up and get Snow Queen from the laundry room and bring her down.

As soon as I walk into the family with her the girls immediately stop what they are saying to fuss over Snow Queen.

"Awe, she's so cute!"

"I love her blue eyes!"

"I love her white paws."

"Can I hold her?"

I hand her over to Abigail, even though I know it won't last. Snow Queen immediately squirms out of her grasp and falls to the floor, which is where she wanted to be in the first place.

I go to the cupboard and get her treats and toys out so

the girls can play with her. We sit on the floor giving Snow Queen all the attention for a while. We run feathers across the floor and when she gets tired of that we try a toy mouse. When she gets tired of the mouse we give her treats. Then she finally climbs in my lap and falls asleep.

"She's an awesome birthday present," Katherine comments.

"She is," I agree.

"How are we going to see your floor routine with her in your lap like that?" Abigail asks.

"Maybe I can move her," I say, gingerly lifting her up and trying to stand at the same time. Of course, I wake her and she is not happy about it. I immediately put her on a pillow on the couch. She stands up, looks at me, and saunters to a different pillow.

"Shall we move these?" Katherine asks, referring to the couches.

We move the two couches, a chair, and a coffee table to the walls at the edge of the room. Snow Queen just looks at us while we move the couch she is sitting on.

Once the room is cleared of furniture I begin to figure out what my pattern will be. Abigail and Katherine plop on the couches and wait.

"Okay, I think I've got it," I say. I hand Abigail my phone. "Here, just hit play. I have it connected to the speaker, already."

She nods, "Tell me when you're ready."

I go to my pretend corner on the other side of the room, raise my arms, and say, "Ready." Abigail hits play and almost instantly my music begins. I do my beginning dance and where I'm supposed to tumble I just walk across the room.

"This is when I tumble," I explain.

"We got that," Katherine says.

I wait for the music in a lunge. When the music catches up to me I continue on with the dance, leap, more dance, and the last tumbling pass. Then I do a terrible turn and do the final dance sequence, my jumps, and ending pose.

When I'm done I look expectantly at my friends.

"That was great!" Abigail says.

"You have some classic ballet in there. Where did you learn to do that?"

"From the ballet classes at the gym. We have a real Madame from the Salt Lake City Ballet."

"I can tell. You even have pique turns in there."

"I do? I don't actually know what that is."

Katherine stands up, "It's this move," she says demonstrating a turn sequence that I have in my routine.

"Oh, what's it called again?"

"Pique turns," she says.

"They're fun," I admit.

"They totally are. Ballet has its moments."

"Let's see it again," Abigail requests.

"Really? You want to see it again?"

"Yes."

"Good, because I'm supposed to practice it a lot," I admit.

I do my routine at least five more times. Katherine and Abigail are much more useful than I thought they would be. They correct me on my pique turns and my one and a half turn. They criticize my arm positions on some of my moves

New Challenges

and they tell me to get my chin up. They could be gymnastics dance teachers someday.

"Can we make up something new now?" Abigail asks.

"Yes, I'm beat," I say, and flop on the couch.

"What song," Katherine asks and starts scrolling through her phone. Pretty soon all of us are looking at music on our phones trying to find a good dance song. We play several for each other but can't seem to decide.

The girls absently start talking about school and homework. I'm exhausted, I'm glad we didn't find a song. I'm happy to sit here and listen to them. Snow Queen sees me and comes over to my lap and curls up.

"Paige, you look a little pale," Abigail says to me.

"I think I'm just tired. I've been going non-stop since last week. I don't know how I'm going to get through practice tomorrow."

"Can you take a day off?" Katherine asks.

"Not really, not this time of year. Unless I'm sick for real. I'm not though; just out of steam I guess."

"She's right. You don't look so good."

"Gee thanks," I say with sarcasm.

"Oh, here's one!" Abigail says, having found the perfect song. Thankfully they've forgotten about me and my exhaustion.

Am I really that pale? I would get up and look in the mirror, but Snow Queen is sitting on me. I didn't think I was pushing myself that hard, but maybe I am.

Katherine agrees that the song Abigail found is perfect and they quickly throw together a routine. I stay on the couch. I blame Snow Queen even though we all know the real reason is I just can't seem to find the energy to get up.

Chapter 21

I'm excited to get to practice and show my teammates my compete floor routine. I'm feeling better than last night, but still kind of off. I have a weird headache and belly ache. I better not be getting sick. I don't have time to be sick. I only have a few weeks before the second and final intrasquad.

We go to bars first and I have a decent practice. Katie is spotting me on flyaways and I'm becoming more comfortable with having her there rather than James. I'm really just piking my flyaway rather than laying out, but it's progress.

"Keep that hollow body position you have when you

let go. Stop bending in the hips," Katies says to me.

I know I'm bending in the hips. I just don't see how I'm going to get around to my feet if I stay straight.

"Why don't you go do a few into the pit. Remember what it feels like. Throw a mat in if it feels good."

I'm happy to go to the pit so I can learn this skill correctly. The downside is the pit bar can get lonely. I readjust my grips as I walk by the beams and across the floor to the pit bar and take a deep breath, this is the only skill I need to have a decent Level 6 bar routine. I can do this. I climb up to the bar, do a few tap swings and a tuck flyaway to warm up.

"What are you working?" Lucy asks walking up. I look at her from my position buried in foam squares.

"Layout flyaways," I answer.

"For a second I thought you were doing double back timers," she replies.

"Yeah, right," I chuckle climbing out. "I have to get the layout first."

"I thought you had your layout?" she questions.

"I sort of do with James. I hold back with Katie," I say quietly as I get out so none of the coaches will hear me.

"I know how hard it is to change coaches," Lucy says with sympathy.

"I can't imagine changing gyms." When Lucy came here she was quiet and never complained. Looking back, it must have been a big change. "Why are you over here?"

"I'm done with my assignment so I get to work double back timers."

"Wow, are you allowed to do that in Level 6?"

"It's not for Level 6 or even Level 7. Katie wants me

to work them for Level 8."

"Do you think it will throw off your layout?" I ask.

"I don't think so. The body positions are so different. I don't think it will make me over rotate my layout."

I wasn't even thinking about over rotating, I was thinking more about forgetting which body position to do. I watch Lucy jump up to the high bar and pump into a long hang kip. Then she stops up in a support position on the high bar, takes a deep breath, casts almost to handstand, swings down and does a nice high tuck flyaway. Instead of landing on her feet she scoops her feet and lands on her back in the pit. Doing one and a quarter flips.

"That looks easy Lucy!" Lucy smiles as she hears Katie from across the gym.

"She doesn't know I did these at camp. I didn't want to say anything in case I forgot how to do them."

"Looks like you remembered."

"Yeah, I'll be able to flip it if she comes over and spots," she says.

"I can't wait to see it," I say and jump up and swing into my flyaway. Inspired by Lucy's beautiful flyaway, I decide to really try to stay hollow for the layout. I tap three times, see my toes, let go, stay hollow, and easily flip to my feet.

"Good Paige, now from a cast!" Katie yells over to me.

"How does she see everything?" I ask Lucy.

"Everything," Lucy agrees.

I eventually do my layout flyaway from a cast in the pit, but it is still a little piked. I think I pike to make sure I get it around. I'm going to have to get more brave on these.

After bars we go to beam and all the girls are doing

full routines while I'm on low beam working handstand back extension rolls.

Katie gets everyone started on their assignment and then comes over to me. "You have a couple of choices on the back extension roll series," Katie says to me.

"What is that?" I ask, curious.

"You can do a handstand step down like you've been doing or you can do a handstand straddle down into in."

"Staddle down?"

"Here let me show you. Shannon Miller did it beautifully in '96," she says, pulling out her phone. She pulls up the routine she is thinking of and shows me. Sure enough a tiny Olympian is doing a perfect handstand. Rather than stepping down out of her handstand she brings it down controlled to a straddled sitting position and immediately rolls back into a back extension roll. Then out of that handstand she does another one.

"She does two!" I exclaim.

"I know, so rare. And she did them perfectly."

"Can I see again?" I ask. She nods and hands me the phone.

"When you're done watching, try some handstand straddle downs on the medium beam. Use a sting mat for your first several."

I take the phone and am mesmerized by Shannon Miller's back extension rolls. I go to the floor and kick up to a handstand and try my press down. I could never press up to handstand, but I did get pretty good at straddling down. When I feel good about that, I go get a sting mat and drag it over to the medium beam and throw it over. When I step up I pause for a second, not sure how this is going to go.

"Do the handstand in front of the mat, then straddle down onto it and roll on it," Katie instructs.

I do as she says and kick up to handstand with my hands on the beam just in front of the mats. I straddle and try to control it down, but at the last second I plop down on the sting mat. I do this a few more times until finally I do one that is controlled and rolling back out of it is easy.

"That's it Paige!" Katie exclaims, "Just like that, do it again!"

Motivated by Katie's excitement I immediately do it again. I'm able to control it down again and roll back.

"Push up into that back extension roll. Don't be shy," Katie says.

"Okay," I say, standing next to the medium beam. My back is aching, I wonder if I jarred it plopping down onto the beam the first few times. "May I get a drink?"

Katie absently nods and I turn to the drinking fountain. I have a water bottle upstairs, but I don't want to go all the way up. I just need a second to see what is going on with my back. I hope I'm not hurt. The ache is deep inside my back, I must have been in less control coming down than I thought. I take a drink and walk a little hoping it will go away. It doesn't go away, but it doesn't hurt so bad that I need to stop either. I go back to my medium beam determined to get this combination.

I climb up, pausing for a moment to think about what I need to do. Tight handstand, control it down, and go right into the back extension roll that I have been doing for over a year. I raise my arms, kick up into a tight handstand, straddle and in a controlled movement lean my shoulders

New Challenges

forward a bit, roll my hips so I straddle down smoothly. As soon as I touch the beam, I roll back and push up into a handstand and fall off to the side.

"That's it! Do you like that way better?" Katie asks me.

"It's faster, so pushing up into the handstand is easier. Controlling it down is hard," I admit.

"You decide which is easier for you," she says. "Try the other way and see."

"Right now?"

"Yes."

I jump up and kick to a handstand, step down, and roll into a back extension roll. It is harder to push up into the handstand because I'm moving slower. I fall off to the side and look at Katie. She looks at me, waiting for me to speak.

"Tough call. The speed of the straddle down helps, but I can't always control it down."

"Keep working both then," she says, turning to the group and yelling that we have five minutes.

I jump up and do a few more before we have to rotate. Katie tells the team to go get a drink and go to floor, then she walks over to me.

"You'll get your beam routine this Saturday," she informs me.

"Do I need to stay after practice?"

"No Melony can come work with you during practice. You'll be able to do routines next week."

"What about my series?" I ask, referring to the handstand back extension roll.

"You can just do the handstand back extension roll with a pause in routines until you're ready to connect it," she comments, unconcerned.

She walks with me to the lobby so I can get a drink. "I know it's all very fast, Paige. You're doing well. You'll find success this season," she says matter-of-factly.

I wish I was as confident.

I look out the parent viewing area as I pass it to the optionals room. The Level 4s and 5s are here, which means James will not be with us on floor. I have to start trusting Katie. She has done nothing to make me feel like she can't spot. In fact, she spots the upper optional girls. I'm just used to James.

I go into the optionals room and over to my locker. The rest of my team is already there, finishing up a quick snack and closing their locker doors. I quickly get out my drink and a sports bar. I take one bite of the sports bar and all of a sudden I don't want it. I can't be sick. Not only am I behind in the gym, but my school is so tough that missing a day or two means a ton of homework. I take a quick sip of water and set it back down then follow my teammates out of the room and back down into the training area.

Katie is ready on floor. There are no upper optional girls in the gym on Wednesdays so we have Katie for the entire rotation.

"Two of each tumbling pass. One routine with your first pass, one routine with your second pass, and one dance through," she announces.

"Paige, I want you to do one dance through, and one routine with one pass. Whichever one you want." I know she is giving me an easier assignment because my routine is new. But I do not have the luxury of several weeks of dance throughs like my teammates.

New Challenges

    The girls spread out to the different corners and Katie announces that someone has to start a routine so we can get through everyone before practice is over. Brooklyn volunteers to start with her dance through while everyone else tumbles.

    I warm up with a round-off back handspring and feel pretty good. Then I do a round-off back handspring back tuck and it is terrible. My set must have been off because I landed really low.

    "Snap down more out of that back handspring and get your chest up for your set," Katie tells me. I nod, grateful for the correction. I knew something was off.

    I go to the corner and wait for a moment while Brooklyn is dancing.

    "That diagonal can go while she is in this corner!" Katie yells at the other corner. "You should know her pattern by now!" she reminds us.

    Aubrey from the opposite diagonal tumbles while Brooklyn dances near my corner. Then Brooklyn runs to the other end of the floor where her tumbling would be and dances along the side of the floor so Savannah in our corner knows to tumble. She does a beautiful layout. When did that get so good? Savannah, Lucy, and Alexis have really improved since we've been with the Level 6s and 7s.

    Brooklyn's music ends and it's my turn to tumble. I think about the exact correction Katie gave me. Usually that works and I can make the correction. To my surprise I do another really low back tuck. It just felt wrong and my back is throbbing. Maybe I really did hurt myself doing those klutzy swing downs on beam.

    "Who wants to go next?" Katie calls out, scrolling

down the gym phone.

"I will!" I volunteer. I have been dying to do my routine for my teammates and my tumbling is a disaster right now anyway.

"Great, Paige it is," she says, finding my music as I walk to my starting corner. My teammates stop tumbling and Katie doesn't yell at them this once. It is an unwritten rule that the gym is allowed to stop for new floor routines. When my music comes on I can tell the entire gym turns to watch. This time I have a full routine to show them.

I have a great time with the music and my ballet moves. I improved a lot last night working with Katherine and Abigail and I am happy to show it off.

When my music ends the gym claps, which surprises me a little.

"Beautiful Paige. Now we just have to get you conditioned in a month to add the tumbling. Who's up?"

Savannah volunteers to go next. Since the gym has seen her routine several times, everyone goes back to work.

I decide to go to front tucks. I don't want to go back to terrible back tucks again. My front tucks are unusually low. What is going on? I get no correction from Katie since she's watching Savannah's dance through.

I finish my three front tucks and I have no choice but to go back to back tucks. Now Alexis is doing her routine. I watch as she moves through her routine and I know when she leaps along the floor that I am safe to take a turn. I run, do my round-off back handspring, back tuck. Only instead of making the back tuck around, I land short and immediately put my hands down, ending on my hands and knees. I sit back on my heels. I feel woozy and out of sorts.

New Challenges

"Paige, are you okay?" I hear Katie ask. She sounds far away. I look up and see her closer to me than I would have guessed.

"Paige?" she asks, putting her hand out to help me up. "You're a little pale, everything all right? Did that one rattle you?"

"I'm off," I say slowly. "Something's wrong."

"Go get a drink and sit down. Did you eat a snack? Did you eat lunch today?" she asks me with her hand still on my arm.

"I think so," I say. Come to think of it, food hasn't sounded good all day and I'm not sure what I've eaten.

"Maya, go get Paige a granola bar from my office and sit her down," she orders, passing me off.

Maya grabs my arm and leads me to one of two chairs in the training area. Once she has me sitting she disappears in the coaches office and comes back out with a granola bar.

She hands it to me and says, "Trust me, you want to eat. I tried it for a while and it just made my gymnastics worse, not better."

"What are you talking about?" I ask, taking the bar she is holding out to me.

"You stopped eating, right? That's why you're landing short and are so pale."

What? I shake my head, "No, that's not it."

"Could have fooled me. Paige, you look great. You're just growing. Don't sabotage yourself, okay?"

"Okay," I agree, even though that's not my problem. Although, to be fair, it did cross my mind these last few weeks. Today wasn't intentional though, I just didn't feel like eating much. I sit and eat my granola bar while I watch my teammates run routines.

"All okay over here?" James asks. The Level 4s and 5s are on beam, right next to where I'm sitting. I nod, embarrassed that everyone thinks I've been starving myself.

He pauses and looks at me for a moment with those sharp gray eyes. "Better take care of yourself if you want to be a high level athlete."

"I will. I promise." He nods and goes back to his team.

I watch the Level 4s and 5s playing around with new skills since they're not in season. Should I have stayed with them? Carmen jumps down from a beam, catches my eye and waves. I give a weak smile and wave back.

I want to get back to my workout, but I feel so gross. I lean forward and put my elbows on my knees and my face in my hands. Maybe I'm just tired. I have worked out every day since Sunday. Usually I would rest on Sunday and Tuesday. I don't feel like I worked that hard on those extra days, but maybe I did. Maybe this is what it means to be in optionals. Hard work. I better keep up if I'm going to compete in the intersquad in a few weeks. I need to finish this workout even if I feel crummy.

I decide to go to the restroom and then get back to work. I stand up quickly and get woozy again. I grab the back of the chair for support and stand still until it passes. Maybe I do need to call my mom. *What a royal bummer*, I think as I walk to the bathroom that is off of the training area. I push open the door debating in my head if I should stay for the rest of the workout or call my mom and go home. I sit down on the toilet and look down and to my

New Challenges

surprise I see bright red blood spots in my underpants. Oh my gosh, my period! What do I do? I don't have any pads with me. Would pads even work in a leotard? I should have put pads in my gym bag. How much more blood is going to come out? Will it make a mess if I go back to practice? I have to go home. I feel awful anyway. I wad up a bunch of toilet paper and stick it in my underwear. I'm grateful I'm wearing black workout shorts today. I stand up and go to the sink to wash my hands. I look in the mirror and see that Katie was right, I am pale. Is all this misery because of my period? The loss of energy and wooziness? The tummy ache? It all makes sense now.

I finish washing my hands, dry them off, and leave the bathroom. There is a girl outside waiting for me. Hopefully I wasn't in there too long. I walk over to Katie.

"How are you feeling?" she asks me when I walk up.

"Not great," I answer honestly. "Can I go home?"

"Of course, get some rest," she says, with real sympathy. She must think I'm either coming down with the flu or I'm starving myself.

I want to get out of here before any of my teammates ask me what's wrong. I quickly turn and go out of the training room and into the lobby. I walk up to the optional room to get my phone and text my mom.

> Me:
> Not feeling well. Can you come get me?
> Mom:
> Of course. What's wrong?
> Me:
> I got my period.

Mom:
>Be right there.

Chapter 22

I look at my phone and for the first time I realize that all women, including my mom, know what this feels like. They are all in on the secret and they don't tell kids. Is everyone caught off guard like me?

I pull out my sweatshirt and sweat pants and throw them on. Then I worry that blood may seep through my black shorts onto my light gray sweat pants. Do I put them on anyway, or leave them off? I take my sweatshirt back off and tie it around my waist. I put my water and snacks in my gym bag, throw it over my shoulder, and shut my locker.

Do the older girls leave pads in their lockers? Or

tampons? I'm tempted to look but then I realize I already know; they must leave supplies here. That's probably why Katie gives the older kids lockers instead of cubbies. I leave the optionals room and quickly walk through the parent viewing area. There are more parents on Wednesdays since the upper optionals aren't here and there's more room in the gym for recreational kids. Thankfully, none of the parents pay attention to me. I make it downstairs and walk through the lobby and outside. I know waiting in the cold December air is not the best idea for a sick kid. I'm not sick . . . I'm . . . I'm . . . a woman.

It actually feels good to stand in the cold. I didn't realize I was heating up in there. I feel my cheeks and they are warm with a small fever. Or is it from panic? Or embarrassment? I'm not sure which. I try to slow down my breathing. I focus on watching the puffs of air as I breathe out into the cold air. The slow breathing calms me. My head feels better, my stomach still feels icky, and my back aches. I'm worried I hurt myself doing those handstand swing downs on beam.

After about ten minutes I see my mom's van round the corner and enter the parking lot. I step closer to the edge of the curb as she pulls up. As soon as the car stops I climb into the front passenger seat.

"I'm so sorry pumpkin. Did you have stuff?"

"No," I say as grumpy as I feel.

"I'm sorry, we should have put some pads in your gym bag."

"I don't see how pads will work. All lumpy under a leo."

"It depends on the pad and how heavy you are. How

heavy is it?" she asks me.

"How should I know? I didn't sit and watch! I just left."

"Okay. We'll figure it out. Start with a medium pad and depending on how fast you go through it we can go bigger or smaller."

"What if I am . . . heavy, as you call it? What do I do at practice?"

"You wear tampons."

"Those seem difficult."

"Paige, there are lots of female athletes who go through what you're going through. They wear tampons and it will feel like you're not even having a period."

"What about the light headedness and tummy ache? That will still remind me," I say surly.

"Do you have a headache?"

"Yes and I got light headed a couple of times. And my tummy hurts."

"Oh pumpkin, I'm sorry. We can go home and make you feel more comfortable."

"I think I hurt my back today, too. Probably because I was feeling off."

"You did?" she asks, flicking a surprised look at me before turning back to the road. I tell her about the back extension roll and how I am trying to connect it to a handstand by swinging down the then rolling back.

"I must have slammed down harder than I thought because it hurts deep inside."

"Your lower back?" she asks.

"Yeah," I say, feeling the ache even more acutely now.

"I think that's cramps from your period."

New Challenges

"In my back?!" I exclaim.

"Yes, you are feeling your uterus."

I think about that for a moment, "At least I'm not hurt then. That's weird it hurts all the way back there. Why does it hurt so bad?"

"Your uterus is squeezing, working for the first time. You're getting sore. Like a sore muscle."

"Does it get better then? If it gets stronger?"

"Yes, actually. Periods usually get easier as you get older. They can be unpredictable for young people," she admits.

I'm silent as I take in all this information. Now I understand why Katherine was so miserable before. I feel bad I wasn't more sympathetic.

We pull into the garage and as soon as we're inside the house my mom disappears and comes back with two boxes of pads (two different sizes) for me to keep in my bathroom. I immediately grab clean underwear and go to my bathroom. I take a pad out of the box, unwrap it, and see that it has paper on the back. I peel off the paper to reveal a sticky strip and I stick it to my underwear. That was easy. I wash up and go back into my bedroom to finish changing. I pull on my fuzziest most comfy sweatpants and throw on my favorite hoodie and head downstairs.

I'm hungry, but nothing sounds good. My back aches and I just want to curl up in a ball. I walk to the couch and do just that. It seems so weird to be home so early. I'm not sure what to do with myself.

"Where's Jason?" I ask my mom.

"At a friend's house." I never thought I would miss him. Now would be the perfect time for his silly magic shows.

"Where's Snow Queen?" I ask.

"She's right here drinking water. I'll bring her to you when you when she's done."

"How long until dinner?"

"A couple of hours. Are you hungry?"

"Not really. Sort of. I don't know," I answer.

"Why don't you call your friends to see if they want to come over and hang out or watch a movie. There's not much to do on a dark winter day," she suggests.

"My friends are all at practice," I comment, rolling my eyes.

"Not all of them. What about your St. Mary's friends? They'll understand."

"My phone's all the way upstairs," I wail.

"No it isn't, silly. You dropped your gym bag by the garage door," my mom says, walking over and picking it up. I watch gratefully as she walks it over to me and drops it in my lap.

"Thanks," I murmur, zipping open my gym bag.

"It's the least I can do," she says and walks away.

I find my phone and text Abigail and Katherine on a group text.

Me:
    Do you guys want to come over?
Katherine:
    Don't you have practice?
Me:
    I left early.

New Challenges

Abigail:
> Everything okay?

Me:
> I guess.

Katherine:
> Tell us.

Me:
> Come over.

Katherine:
> What can we bring?

Me:
> Something that will make my stupid cramps go away.

Abigail:
> You got your period today!

Katherine:
> Welcome to womanhood!

Me:
> Gee, thanks. Just come over.

Abigail:
> I know what to bring.

Katherine:
> Abigail, can you come get me? My mom's not home.

Abigail:
> You are close enough to walk.

Katherine:
> But I don't want to.

Abigail:
> Fine, see you in 5.

I set my phone down and lean my head back. They

distracted me from my pain while I was texting them. Maybe my mom is right, I need to hang out with friends. I hear my mom walking back in and she has a blue square of fabric in her hand that has a electrical cord attached to it. She goes to the wall next to me, plugs it in, and says, "Sit up."

I sit up and ask, "What are you doing?"

"Giving you a hot pad for your back," she says, as she slips it between the couch and my lower back. "Now lean back onto it." I do as she says.

"I don't feel anything," I say.

"Give it a sec," she says. "It will help. Here," she says, holding out a pill for me.

"What is this?"

"Ibuprofen. It will help with your headache and back pain. I promise."

I nod, I'll take all the help I can get. "Will you please get me water?" I ask as nicely as I can. I know I'm pushing my luck with being a spoiled lazy child, but I really, really, don't want to move away from this chair.

"Of course, thanks for asking nicely," she says and goes to get me the water. I sink back into the chair and adjust the hot pad for a minute.

"Ooh, I feel the warmth now, it does fell good," I say, leaning back into the hot pad.

I feel like a big baby. I never knew a period came with so much discomfort. They didn't tell us that in health class. Come to think of it, they didn't tell us nearly enough in health class. I am starting to understand the value of girlfriends. I'm glad Grace answered my questions and wasn't embarrassed to talk to me about it.

My mom hands me a glass of water. I take it from her, swallow the pill, and hand it back to her.

"Keep it here," she says setting it down on the coffee table next to me.

"What else is going to change?" I ask quietly.

"You'll probably fill out more, keep growing," she says.

"What do you mean by 'fill-out'?" I ask. Aunt Jennifer used that phrase, too.

"You know, develop more in your chest, your hips may widen a little, your muscle may bulk up a bit."

"I don't want to be bigger," I wail.

"Paige, it's okay; you're growing up," she reminds me.

"It's not okay. Gymnasts are supposed to be small," I point out.

"Says who? Have you seen the college girls lately? They are regular sized people. Super strong fit people, but still regular."

"They're all 5'2"," I counter.

"But they are *women* who are 5'2". What gave you this idea that you have to be small?"

"I don't know," I say toying with the cord on my heating pad. "I guess because my teammates are small. And it was easier when I was small. I can't do a back tuck anymore," I try to explain.

"You're changing fast, I'm sure you just need to adjust."

I don't say anything to that. I don't know what to say. Adjusting is easier said than done. Thankfully the doorbell rings, ending our conversation.

Abigail and Katherine come in with what feels like

boundless energy.

"You look like crap," Katherine says.

"Katherine!" Abigail chides.

"It's okay. We're here to save the day!" she announces holding up a heating pad.

"Got it," I say. "But thanks."

"Your mom is on it," she says.

Katherine sits on the coffee table and faces me while Abigail takes the chair next to me. Katherine plunks down a canvas bag and starts pulling out junk food.

"We don't know what your PMS foods are yet so we brought everything."

"PMS?" I ask.

"Premenstrual Syndrome."

"Why pre? The uncomfortable part is happening now."

"For some people it's a few days before," Abigail says.

"What is it for you guys?" I ask.

"During," Abigail says.

"Both before and during," Katherine admits.

"Let's see, we brought you potato chips," she says pulling them out of her bag, "chocolate, and red licorice. We don't know if you crave salt, sugar, or chocolate."

I think about it a moment. Nothing sounded good earlier, but now the chips look amazing.

"The chips," I say.

"Salty it is," she says handing them over.

"Oh and we brought you this," Abigail says, pulling out a flier and handing it to me.

I take it and see it's a flier from health class that they printed out. "Your Body and Your Menstruation," I read. "You guys are hilarious," I say, setting it down. Although, secretly, I might read it later. Katherine stands up and walks over to the couch across from us.

"So you couldn't make it through practice today, huh?" Katherine asks.

"No," I say. "I don't know how I'm going to go tomorrow either. And I need to go. It seems like growing is making me worse."

"Dance can be like that," Abigail pipes up. "It's not that you are worse. You just have to readjust your balance and timing for your new body. Your muscles remember the skills."

I nod. It's good advice, but gymnastics seems so much harder to adjust to than dance. I tell them about my tumbling pass and how I feel slow and off.

"And I'm nowhere near getting my flyaway," I admit. When I say it out loud all of sudden I can feel a wave of strong emotion wash though me.

"What's a flyaway?" Abigail asks.

"I don't know . . . " I start, but choke on my own tears. "I don't know if I can do this." The tears that came out of nowhere start streaming down my face. "Why am I crying?"

"Oh, honey, it's just all part of it," Abigail says like an old woman. She grabs the bag they brought and produces a box of tissues and hands it to me.

The absurdity of them knowing I would need a box of tissues make me smile a little as I take the box from her. I open the box and can't seem to get the first tissue out which for some reason frustrates me, making me cry further.

"I can't get it!" I yell, in frustration and throw the box at Abigail. She catches it, pulls out the first tissue and hands it to me. I can tell my friends are trying not to laugh. "What?" I growl.

"You just have it bad."

"Have what bad?"

"Just all the symptoms that go along with getting your period."

"I don't think so. I think I'm just under a lot of pressure to do a level I clearly have no business doing," I say, falling deeper into my self-pity.

"Who is pressuring you?" Katherine asks.

"No one. Me. My coaches. Maybe. I don't know. I decided to do this by January and it's almost January," I finally explain.

"Seems like everyone is just helping you because you said you wanted to do it."

"Shut up," I say, making them laugh, even though it's not that funny.

The girls stay for another hour or so keeping me company. My emotions get more under control when we talk about other things, like school, clothes, and their dance classes. They show me some funny TikTok videos to cheer me up and it does help.

I learn to keep my mind focused on them and what they are talking about because anytime I think about gymnastics I start to feel the tears well up. I really don't want to cry again.

When Katherine's mom texts that she was coming to get them, I feel drained.

"Keep the bag, you can restock it and give it back to me when I need it," Abigail says. I nod and start to get up to walk them to the door.

"No need," Katherine says, pushing me back down. "Stay in your cocoon with your hot pad."

I sit back down, "Thanks guys."

"See you tomorrow!" Abigail sings as she walks down the hall to my front door.

"Congratulations on becoming woman!" Katherine tosses over her shoulder, making me grin. I'm lucky to have them as friends.

"What makes you a woman?" Jason asks, walking through the front door. I have no idea what to say to him.

"She's thirteen now," my mom says, saving me from any explanation. "That was sweet of your friends to come over and keep you company." She says, pulling out a TV tray and setting it in front of me.

"I can eat in here?" I ask surprised. My mom is a big stickler for dinner time as a family.

"Dad's working late and you don't look like you want to move. I figured, just this once." I watch her go back into the kitchen and come back with a bowl of soup and bread and set it down on the tray.

"I'm not sick," I comment looking at the bowl.

My mom straightens up and looks at me, "You don't have to be sick to enjoy soup on a cold winter day."

Good point. I nod and whisper, "Thanks." Because even though I'm not sick, I sure don't feel myself.

Chapter 23

The hard wooden chairs that are attached to our desks seem extra hard today. I squirm in my seat and cannot get comfortable. My back hurts like crazy and I'm starting to get a headache. I'm so worried that the pad I'm wearing won't work that I'm wearing gymnastics shorts under my plaid skirt. I used to wear the shorts under my skirt all the time when I did gymnastics at recess. When I started sixth grade I didn't need to anymore because we no longer had recess.

Last night before bed, I pulled out the pamphlet Katherine and Abigail brought over as a joke. I read the entire thing to see if I ignored information in fifth grade when we had the maturation class at school. The pamphlet

New Challenges

explained all the things that are happening in my body and how I would continue to change and how I need deodorant. But it didn't say anything about all the weird symptoms. Maybe that's why Katherine and Abigail found the pamphlet funny, it only tells half the story. They need an asterisk in there that says *for all useful information talk to your besties.*

 I manage to make it through the day and as soon as I get home I toss my backpack on the floor and fall to the couch. How can I possibly do gymnastics feeling this way?

 My mom finds me curled up on the couch when she comes home in time to take me to practice. Usually I am dressed and ready for practice when she gets home and we run out the door.

 "Maybe you should stay home today," she says.

 I lift my head and look at her. I agree with her, I should stay home. I'm not sure how I'm going to catch up at this rate and that thought bothers me as I lay my head back down, "Yeah," I say.

 "I'll text Katie," she says.

 "Just tell her I'm sick," I mumble. I wouldn't put it past my mom to tell her exactly what is going on. That thought embarrasses me. I think about it for a moment. I guess Katie knows what I'm going through. It would be more embarrassing if she had to call James.

 I hear my mom come back in the room, "I sent Jason over to play with Will and Dad is going to be home late again so it's just us girls." She sits down next to me and starts rubbing my back. "I'm sorry it's so painful for you." I don't say anything and after a moment she gets up again, "I'm going to get you an ibuprofen. When was the last time you had one?" she asks me.

"Yesterday," I mumble.

"Well, no wonder. Let's help you a bit with your cramps," she leaves again and comes back with a little maroon pill and a glass of water. I sit up and take it without question. "Do you want to watch a movie?"

"How am I ever going to catch up at the gym if I stay home to hang out with friends and watch movies with you?" I ask.

My mom starts rubbing my back again, "It's not always going to be like this. You'll learn how to manage your body. What activities make you feel better, which healthy foods help, that kind of thing."

I think about this for a minute. "Sometimes I wish I was a boy," I admit.

"I think all girls think that at some point. Especially when it comes to their period and childbirth. We can't change it, so I like to think about what I like about being a girl," she says.

"The clothes," I smile.

"And make-up," she says.

"We can wear dresses or pants."

"We have good friendships."

"We have better hair," I say making my mom laugh.

"See, it's not all bad," my mom says. "What do you want to watch?" she asks me.

"On a week night?" I ask. Usually we are not allowed movies on week nights.

"Of course, finish your homework first and then, yes, let's watch something fun. It's just us girls, so we can watch whatever we want," she says with enthusiasm. Jason usually picks the movies on our Friday night movie night, so this is a fun treat.

"Let's see what Rom-Coms they have," I say, getting into the spirit.

We pick a romantic comedy that was released straight to streaming. It's a cute show, but my mind keeps wandering back to gymnastics. How am I possibly going to catch up if I have to take several days off each time I get my period?

"When do you think I'll start to feel better?" I ask my mom.

"The worst part is the first three days. Hopefully by tomorrow you'll feel better."

"We don't even have practice tomorrow," I sulk.

"Then you will for sure be able to go on Saturday," she predicts.

This satisfies me enough to focus on the rest of the movie.

My mom was right, I do feel better today. It's Saturday and I haven't been to the gym since Wednesday, when I left practice before it ended. My only concern is that I'm still bleeding enough that I need a big pad or a tampon. A small pad, or panty liner, would work in a leo, but I think I need more protection than that. Thank goodness our gym allows workout shorts over our leos whenever we want. The only exception is we have to take them off for intrasquads and meets.

My mom bought me a box of tampons, knowing it was one of the few answers for athletes. I told her I don't know how to use them and she told me to read the directions in the box. So that's what I'm doing now. I have the directions spread out on the bathroom counter. The instructions include pictures. While the pictures are totally something Katherine and Abigail would make fun of, I'm glad to have them. I take a deep breath and decide to try.

After three failed attempts I'm frustrated and trying not to cry. How hard can this be? She makes it look easy in the picture. I start panicking that I'm going to be late for gymnastics and that makes everything worse. A few more attempts and I throw the instructions across the small room and bury my face in my hands.

"Paige, are you okay in there?" I hear my mom asking through the door. I must have been in here for ages.

"No!" I yell back. "I can't do it!"

There is a pause. "Can you wear a light pad? One of the panty liners?"

"No!" I yell back in frustration.

"What do you want to do? Keep trying or skip today?" she asks.

Skip today? I can't miss another day. I feel good, small cramps and more energy than I've felt in days. I look up at the ceiling. I really hate this. I walk over and pick up the instructions again.

"I don't want to skip," I yell in frustration.

"Okay, Paige, try to relax. Take your time. It's no big deal to be late once in a while. You can do this."

New Challenges

I take some deep breaths and try to relax. I can do this. I can do back flips for crying out loud, I should be able to do this. I take a deep breath and clam myself down. I try one last time and, to my surprise, I'm successful. My mom is right. Once the tampon is in, it doesn't feel like anything. I quickly wash up, shove the instructions back in the box, and throw the box under the sink.

"I'm ready!" I announce.

"You did it?" my mom asks.

"I did it," I say with pride opening the bathroom door. For once I think I just did something before Katherine and Abigail. I'm pretty sure neither of them have worn a tampon yet. I probably wouldn't have either if I wasn't determined to go to practice today. "Am I going to feel it?" I ask my mom.

"You shouldn't," she says. "The biggest thing is to remember to take it out."

"How do I know when to take it out?"

"Take it out after three or four hours or when it's full."

"How do I know when it's full?"

"You will start spotting. Are you wearing a panty liner?"

"A what?"

"One of the lighter pads," she says, walking into the bathroom and grabbing one of the boxes. "You wear one of these with it."

Without a word I take the box from her and shut myself back into the backroom.

Chapter 24

My teammates are happy to see me when I show up for Saturday morning practice. I didn't realize they were worried about me when I abruptly left on Wednesday. I'm sticking to the story that I had a little tummy ache and no one seems to question it or care. They're just glad I'm back.

As soon as we finish warming up Melony pulls me out of the group to teach me my beam routine. She took dance movements and poses from my floor routine and choreographed them into my beam routine. She lets me choose if I want to do my back extension roll first thing or after a leap pass. I decide to do the leap pass first, then the

New Challenges

back extension roll. After that I just have jumps and a full turn. The routine was fast to learn but I'm not sure I'm actually going to remember it. I ask Melony to record me doing it on my phone so I can go home and memorize it. Everyone else is doing routines that seem second nature to them. I want mine to get like that. Melony and I stay over on the beams working on my routine for the entire bars rotation. While I need to work my flyaway, I need a beam routine more.

"What's your dismount?" Melony asks me after watching me do a full dance through of my new routine.

"Front tuck."

"How about a dance through with the mount and dismount?"

"Let me warm up the front tucks," I say. I do about three front tucks off the end of the beam. They are a pretty simple skill if you can do front tucks on floor. The only hard part is being ready for the landing. I feel good about knowing where I am and glad I have a new dismount this easily.

When the bars rotation (that I missed altogether) is over, my teammates join me on beam. Katie announces five stuck routines and five of everything we fall on. It dawns on me that I can actually do this assignment today.

"Paige," Katie calls over to me, "do a cartwheel where the round-off goes."

"We didn't put in a round-off," I admit.

"Are you planning to learn it?"

Not in less than three weeks! "Yes."

"Then choreograph it in and do a cartwheel for now. When you get the round-off you can replace the cartwheel."

I stand there a little dumbfounded. There are now two skills in my routine that I am nowhere near doing and I don't know where to put the round-off. Or cartwheel really, because that is what it's going to be for a while.

"Where should I put the round-off?" I squeak.

"Melony!" Katie yells past a few beams to where Melony is helping Lucy.

Melony looks up and Katie yells, "Can you add a round-off to Paige's routine?"

Melony looks at me, nods, and goes back to helping Lucy. When she is done she comes over to me.

"A round-off in the routine, huh?" she says walking up to me by the low beams.

"Guess so," I sulk.

"It's actually smart because then you don't have to rework the entire routine when you get that skill." I don't say anything because rearranging dance seems minimal. "This is optionals, you can change your routine whenever you need to."

I do like that, but just when I feel like I have a handle on Level 6, I get pushed to do more than I feel like I can do.

"Don't look so down. You can do a cartwheel right?"

"Of course," I say. A cartwheel was in the Level 4 routine, she knows I can do it.

"Then this is no big deal. Where should we put it? In the end? After your series?"

I think about it for a moment, "After the series," I confirm. Melony does some movements on the low beam, trying to figure out how I can gracefully move in and out of the cartwheel. Then she turns to me and teaches to me what she just created. Then I put it all together doing a dance through on low beam.

"That's exactly it. Want me to record it?" she asks and I nod and run over and grab my phone that was sitting on a panel mat nearby. "After this you should go put your phone away before someone steps on it," she comments, taking the phone from me.

I do the new dance through on the low beam while Melony records it. On the first try I totally forgot the new section she taught me. Melony is nice about it and shows it to me again. I try again, this time I get it right and Melony gets it on video.

"Got it. Now go put your phone away and do five more so you can start to commit it to memory. Then work on your series," she instructs.

I do as she says and run up and put my phone away. It feels good to have a beam routine. Now I can finally participate in the all-around at the next intrasquad. *Not if you don't have all your skills* a rude voice in my head reminds me. That makes me run back downstairs faster so I have time to work my series on beam before we rotate to floor.

I end up doing my five dance throughs on high beam and both Savannah and Brooklyn comment on how pretty my routine is, which is nice of them. I was also able to get a few tries of my handstand swing down to back extension roll. I'm still doing it on the medium beam with the sting mat thrown over the beam. I think I can actually get this skill in the next few weeks. It definitely seems easier than a back walkover back handspring, even though everyone else says the opposite.

By the time the beam rotation is over, I'm tired of beam. I've been here for two rotations and I'm ready to go to floor.

On floor my back tucks feel better and I'm happy I can finally participate in the assignment with everyone else. As I walk by the mirror to get from one corner to the other I am surprised at what I see. I feel like my legs are so much bigger than they used to be. Thicker. When did that happen? I will myself not to stop and stare as I walk by and see a person I don't even recognize.

I get to my corner and I can't seem to concentrate. I decide to do my front tuck first. I'm not in a good place mentally to do back tumbling right now. I'm rattled by what I saw. I take a deep breath and run and do a nice front tuck.

"Paige are you ready?" I hear Katie yell over to me. I look over and nod to her. "Are you starting with the dance through or the last pass set?" she asks.

"Last pass," I tell her. I love that in optionals my last pass can be my front tumbling where compulsories my hardest pass, the back tumbling, was always at the end of the routine. Now I can switch it up and do my layout (or back tuck) in the first pass and my front tuck in the last pass.

I hardly need to be warmed up to do a routine with a front tuck at the end, which is probably why Katie called on me to go early on. The Level 7s need more time to warm up their passes.

I stand in the corner and wait for my music to start. I enjoy the dance and try to show off my movements. I'm surprised to find myself a bit winded as I stand in the corner before my front tuck. I take a deep breath, run, punch, do my front tuck and barely land it. I do my end dance and when I hit the ending pose I'm shocked at how tired I am. Without asking I walk over and get a drink.

That was hard. Harder than I expected. Then I smile to myself because I am doing routines.

At the end of practice I'm waiting in the lobby for my mom when Katie walks up, "I told your mom to come a few minutes late because I'd like to speak with you. Come on in," she says motioning for me to go into the coaches' office.

She wants to speak with me? Oh no, what if she has decided I shouldn't compete this season?

I enter the office with a horrible feeling settling over me. All this hard work to sit out this season. She pulls her chair from around the desk and motions for us to sit next to each other.

"How are things going Paige?" she asks me.

"Fine," I answer, not sure what she is asking.

"What happened at your last practice?"

"My last practice?" I ask, not sure what she is talking about. My last practice I did everything I was told.

"When you left early. Everything okay?" she presses.

I am not about to tell her I got my period so I just nod.

"Are you eating well?" she continues.

I nod again.

"Paige, you look wonderful and healthy. I hope you are not cutting back on your eating because you don't like how you are changing."

I'm a little offended she thinks I'm not eating, but she hit a bit of a chord on the part about me not liking how I'm changing.

"I'm eating." I say. She looks at me and so I confess, "but I don't like how I'm changing."

"Why not? It's all perfectly normal," she reminds me.

"Not for gymnasts," I say, starting to choke up. "They are little and cute."

"What gymnasts are you talking about?" she asks.

"Savannah, Lucy, Alexis, ... and the old version of me," I crack out, starting to cry.

"Oh, Paige, you can't do that," she says, reaching over and putting her hand over mine. "You are comparing yourself to young girls. You are becoming a woman. There are lots of grown women who are successful gymnasts." I sniff and nod, even though I'm not sure I believe her.

She stands up and shuffles through her desk and pulls out a gymnastics magazine. "Look at our Olympic Team. Grown women," she says, holding the magazine out to me. I sit up and look at the picture she is holding out. She is right. I wipe a tear off my face. Those girls are my size or bigger. "I know the stereotype for gymnastics has historically been that gymnasts must be small and prepubescent to be successful. That is just not the case anymore. These girls have proved that. The college girls have proved that. Look over here, look at these posters," she says, walking over to the wall that has four college posters on it. "Stand up and look at them, Paige," she orders.

I stand up and walk up to the wall. I examine the Utah poster, then I walk over to the BYU poster, then Utah State, and Southern Utah. The gymnasts in the pictures all have broad shoulders, breasts, muscled arms, and strong thick legs. They are beautiful. Their skin is clear and their smiles are bright. They seem comfortable in their intricate sparkling team leotards.

"They're pretty," I say.

"Yes, and that is what you are becoming. A beautiful fit strong woman. You cannot compare yourself to children."

I nod. I don't say anything because for some reason the tears are coming back. The silence stretches between us. Finally, Katie adds, "So please let yourself grow and keep eating healthy, okay?"

I turn and look at her, "I promise I'm eating. But thank you for showing me these pictures." She stands up and walks over to me and gives me a big hug. I swallow my tears and hug her back.

Chapter 25

By Sunday my period is over and I feel lighter than I have felt all week. I can't wait to get back into the gym to learn my series on beam, my layout flyaway on bars, and my layout on floor. The list is intimidating, but I think I can do it. I have seen how much Alexis, Lucy, and Savannah have improved since we moved up to Level 6 and I think I'm only slightly behind them. It's a bit embarrassing to be behind kids who are two years younger than me. That's how gymnastics is sometimes. I mean, Maya is older than everyone else and she doesn't seem to mind. It's also weird to not be the leader anymore. Peyton and Maya definitely are the leaders of Level 6 and 7. Maybe when they move up to Level 8 next year and my old teammates move up from

New Challenges

Level 5, I can be the leader again.

    I look out my bedroom window at the wind and gray clouds. I miss my old teammates. Savannah is having a Christmas Party Friday night with all the Level 6s and some of the 5s. I'm looking forward to it. The only thing that would make it better was if Katherine and Abigail were there. It's a bummer how school friends and gym friends are separate. Unless you are lucky like Savannah and Trista, who go to the same school.

    I spend the day catching up on homework. My homework isn't intended for me to do all in one day at the end of the week. I have been so busy with gymnastics, that that has been the only way to keep up.

    After several hours I'm finally done with homework and I think about texting Katherine and Abigail. But I don't think I can handle all their chatter today. I decide to text Grace. I wish the farm was closer. It seems like the perfect place to be on a quiet cold day like today. The farm makes me think of Snow Queen and I call for her. She is usually active in the early morning, but a bit sleepy this time of day. I wander out of my room looking for her in her favorite sleeping places. I find her in the family room sleeping in a ray of sun coming through the window. Smart little kitty. I sit down next to her and lean against the couch. She wakes when she sees me, stretches, and rolls over to show me her belly. I pet her belly and she stands up and crawls in my lap. Then she kneads my legs for a moment and finally lays down. I pet her and enjoy the warmth with her. I notice her coat is, in fact, turning gray like Grace said it would. She's not as cute as she was even a few weeks ago. I sigh, it's a bummer to grow up.

I think about how my week went as I prepare for Savannah's party. The week flew by both at the gym and at school. At St. Mary's we have several projects we have to finish before the Christmas break and at the gym we are all trying to put our routines together before our intersquad held just before Christmas. I'm just glad I have routines to do at all. Katie hasn't said anything to me, so I assume I'm allowed to compete in the all-around at the intersquad.

I step into my only winter dress and reach around and zip it as far as I can. I stand in front of the mirror debating how I want to do my hair. It would be fun to keep it down since my teammates never see it that way. Savannah told us this party would be fancy and to wear a dress, or at least sparkles. I smile to myself as I pick up a sparkly head band. I think I will do both.

I step into my black ballet flats and go find my mom so she can zip me. I find her in the kitchen sitting down, peeling an orange. She looks up when I walk in.

"Don't you look beautiful," she says, setting down her orange on her napkin.

"I couldn't zip it all the way," I say, walking to her so she can help me. I turn around as she wipes her hands on the napkin, stands up, and faces my zipper. When she zips it, she gets stuck where I did, at my mid back.

"Pumpkin, I don't think I can get this to zip."

"What? No way, I just got it this last spring in the post season sale."

"I know, but you have grown so much."

"Taller, yeah, but wider?"

"Let me try again," she says, bringing the zipper down and tugging on the dress near my waist to make the zipper perfectly straight before she tries again. "Hold this," she says to me. I reach around to my back and pull the dress down and hold it straight. I feel my mom pull the sides together as close as she can. She slowly zips it up and I can feel it getting very tight as she passes my lat muscles. Then it gets easier as she gets to my shoulder blades. I let out a breath when she gets the zipper all the way up.

"That may not hold," she says, making me feel like a cow. "Why don't you bring a back-up dress? One of your summer ones you have that is stretchy jersey material."

"Because it's a winter Christmas party," I point out.

"Maybe bring a pair of jeans and a fancy sweater?" she suggests.

"Can I pick something out and leave it in your car? If something happens you can bring it to me?"

She pauses for a moment so I give her my best pleading expression. "Oh, alright. As much as I hate driving up and down the hill for no reason, I will do it for you. And it's just a precaution. Now that you are in the dress, it looks like it fits."

"It pulls really tight if I move my arms forward," I say, bringing my arms up and in front of me. I feel the seams straining.

"Then don't do that, silly. Now go get your back-up

clothes," she says.

Back-up clothes. When I bought this dress last spring I never dreamed it wouldn't fit this winter. I go to my room and grab my favorite jeans and my only sparkly sweater. I haven't worn it since last Christmas, but it's stretchy material, so it will fit.

I take one more look in the mirror. I look nice. I don't look as crammed into the dress as I feel. I look at the jeans and sweater in my hand and decide I can wear it with the same shoes. I find my mom again who is waiting by the garage door with her purse and keys in her hand.

"Ready?" she asks.

"Ready," I say. I follow her into the garage, climb into the front seat of the car and throw my clothes in the back.

We drive mostly in silence, my mom goes over a few rules about manners that I already know. I'm trying not to move and rip my dress before we get there.

When we arrive, my mom walks me to the door, which she doesn't need to do.

"I want to say hi to Debbie. I'd like to thank her," I roll my eyes, but don't say anything as she follows me up the walk. Thankfully their driveway and path to the door are shoveled because my ballet flats aren't really made for snow.

When we get to the door Savannah answers it. She looks darling in a white tulle dress with rhinestones dotting the skirt.

"Welcome!" she says, and I can tell she is already having the time of her life.

"Hi Savannah," my mom says, "is your mom around?"

Savannah nods, looks over her shoulder, and motions

her mom to the door. Debbie walks up and enjoys the small talk and thank yous from my mom as I walk in.

"Bye pumpkin, see you in a few hours!" I wave goodbye and she leaves, taking my back-up clothes with her.

After she leaves I finally take in the room. The living room just off of the entry way is where the girls are sitting around a beautiful tree with red, blue, and gold bulbs. Trista, Carmen, and Marissa are sitting on one couch and Lucy and her sister, Rose, are sitting on the other. I walk over and take a seat by Lucy.

"Hi Lucy," I say quietly.

"Are we the only 6s who are going to be here?" she asks me.

"I imagine they will all be here," I point out. "But you know the others from the fall," I remind her.

"I do, of course I do. I just wasn't on the Level 5 team for very long before I moved up and these girls know each other really well."

"They do, they have been training together for years."

"Did you see the tree?" she asks me, changing the subject.

I look at it more closely, and I see that the theme is gymnastics. There are ornaments of gymnasts, grips, and trophies. The gold bulbs have a design on them making them look like a gold medal. Some of Savannah's medals are looped over branches, adding to the gymnastics theme.

"Perfect for this crowd," I say, relaxing Lucy a little.

Savannah comes in and sets down a tray of crackers and cheese saying, "Have a little snack you guys, and when everyone gets here, we'll start."

"Start what?" Lucy whispers to me.

I shrug, "Knowing Debbie, it will be good."

We hear the doorbell ring and Savannah flounces to the door to greet Alexis. The moms chat for a moment while Alexis comes in and takes off her coat. She is in a darling dress of midnight blue with little cap sleeves and a square neck line. I look around at everyone and I love that Savannah told us to dress up. I rarely get to see these girls in school clothes, much less in fancy clothes.

Before Debbie has time to shut the door Riley and Victoria arrive. The moms talk while Savannah greets them. "I'm so happy you guys came!" She grabs Victoria's arm and pulls her in. "You guys know Victoria and Riley, right?"

"We know them from PNO," Trista says.

"I'll remind you of names anyway. This is Trista, Carmen, and Marissa. And you know these guys," she says gesturing to Lucy and I. "Oh, do you know Rose? Rose is Lucy's sister."

Victoria and Riley say a quiet hello and we make room on the couch for them to sit.

"What's your favorite event?" Trista asks them, breaking the ice. The girls easily start talking about gymnastics and I can see Savannah visibly relaxing. She must have been worried about mixing these two teams.

When Debbie shuts the door she turns to us, "You girls look so cute. Let's get a picture before we start." She lines us up on the stairs so each of us can be seen. The girls are excited and a little chaotic. I notice Marissa is the one to settle them down. We finally get a good picture and then Savannah sits us down to tell us about our game.

"I have names of famous people on these sticky labels.

New Challenges

You each get one on your back and you have to figure out who you are. You can only ask yes or no questions, like, 'Am I an Olympian?' stuff like that. And you can only ask one question to each person. After one question you have to find someone else. There's a prize for whoever guesses their person first and smaller prizes for second and third. I promise you will love them!"

The girls all start talking at once and Savannah and her mom are trying to figure out how to get us our sticky notes on our back without anyone seeing the names. They also want us all starting at the same time so it's fair.

"We could line up like march-in and you could put all the sticky labels on us and we start at the same time," Marissa suggests.

"Great idea, Marissa," Debbie says. Then she turns to the rest of us. "Girls, line up shoulder to shoulder like you are being announced before a meet."

"Do you want us small to tall?" Riley asks, making us laugh.

"Sure, why not?" Debbie says.

We shuffle around for a minute and in a shockingly quick amount of time we are standing small to tall, shoulder to shoulder. I am on the end as the tallest. It has been a while since I've been the tallest. I look down the row at all the girls in their Christmas party dresses. They are all thin and petite. I bet none of them had trouble zipping up their dress today.

Savannah steps forward with her sticky labels ready to give us each a name and her mom stops her, "Don't you want to play?" she asks.

"No, I'll help people," she says, and begins to walk

along our line, peeling off stickers and sticking them on our backs.

As soon as Savannah passes Trista I see her lean back and look at the stickers on both people next to her.

"They're all gymnasts!" Trista exclaims. This admission makes me feel much better about the game. I don't know famous people like Katherine and Abigail do. I do know gymnasts. Savannah finally gets to me and sticks a label on my back.

"Okay, go!" Savannah says. Girls immediately start asking each other questions.

"Am I an Olympian?"

"Am I on the current national team?"

I hear all these questions when Carmen turns to me, "Am I an elite or college gymnast?" I lean over and look at the sticky on her back. Peng-Peng Lee. She was both.

"You have to ask me a yes or no question," I remind her.

"Was I a college gymnast?" she asks.

"Yes," I confirm.

"Was I a college gymnast?" I ask.

She looks at the name on my back and pauses. "Um, not was," she says.

"Currently I'm a college gymnast?" Since I didn't ask a yes or no question she just gives me a little smile.

Hmm, a new college gymnast, so she didn't get famous that way. Maybe a recent Olympian.

I walk over to Trista, "Am I an Olympian?" I ask her.

She looks at my back. "Sadly no, but you should have been."

"Trista!" Savannah yells at her for giving me an extra

New Challenges

clue.

"What? I can't help it, she should have," Trista justifies unapologetically.

"Ask me a question," I tell Trista, so she doesn't get in further trouble and disqualified from our game. As she's thinking of a question I turn her and look at her back. Jordyn Wieber.

"Let's see, I know I'm an Olympian. Did I win a gold medal?" she asks.

"Yes."

"Team or individual?" she follows up.

"You have to ask someone else."

"Oh yeah," she turns to Alexis, "did I win an all-around gold medal in the Olympics?"

Alexis looks and she says, "Nope. sorry."

"Hmm, team medal then," Trista thinks aloud.

I smile to myself. She'll get it soon. I better focus and think about my gymnast. She's not an Olympian, but she is in college now.

I turn to Alexis, "Did I go to worlds?" I ask.

She turns me, reads my label and says, "You sure did."

Worlds doesn't really narrow it down. This is hard.

"Can I do a triple double?" Victoria asks me. The only females that can do a triple doubles are Simone Biles and Jade Carey. I look at her label: Jordan Chiles.

"No," I say. She is close. Jordan was on the same team as Simone and Jade. I need to think of a good question. All I know is I was at worlds.

"Did I win the all-around at worlds?" I ask her.

"Yes," she confirms. I won worlds but I'm not an Olympian so I'm not Simone. *Think Paige think.* Other gymnasts won worlds before Simone came along.

"Did my floor routine go viral?" I hear someone ask.

"Am I a college coach now?" someone else asks.

They are asking good questions. Then it pops in my head. Morgan Hurd won worlds when Simone took a year off.

"Do I wear glasses?" I ask Rose.

"Yes!" she says.

"Am I Morgan Hurd?" I ask Carmen.

"Yes! Paige got it! Paige got hers!" she yells.

"Everyone stop for a second!" Savannah yells and the girls stop chatting and look over. "We need to see if Paige won and if she did we can keep going for second place.

Savannah walks over to me. "Who do you think you are?" she asks.

"Morgan Hurd."

"Paige is first place winner! You guys can keep going for second." The girls start frantically asking questions again. Savannah looks at me, "You can still answer their questions. That's what I'm doing; it's fun."

"Did you think of all the names?" I ask her.

"My mom and I did."

I nod and Alexis walks up to me with a question, "Am I an announcer?" she asks. I look, Nastia Lukin.

"Yes," I say.

"Am I Nastia Lukin?" she asks.

"Yes!"

"We have second place!" Savannah yells and the room gets more frantic as the girls are getting closer to knowing their gymnasts. I smile, this was a good idea. Only these girls would be able to answer yes or no questions about gymnasts.

"Am I a mom?" I hear someone ask.

"Yes."

"Am I Chelsea Memel?" she asks.

"Yes!"

"Am I an Olympic All-Around Champion?"

"Yes!"

"Am I Suni Li?"

"Yes!"

The third place winner sounded like a tie to me. The game is technically over, so girls start giving each other huge hints.

"You were an Olympian, but not for the US. But you did college in the US."

"Wait, what? I have no idea."

"Yes you do. Think about it."

"Where did I do college."

"No way that's way too easy."

"The game is over!"

"Fine, UCLA."

"Oh! Peng-Peng!"

The girls are so excited when they guess their gymnast even with heavy hints and more than yes or no questions. Once everyone guesses their gymnast the girls settle down and Savannah gives us our prizes. I get a gift bag with hair ties, wrist bands, and a key chain with a gymnast on it. Leave it to Savannah's mom to make everything gymnastics themed. She knows this group.

I look up from my gift bag and see everyone is talking about the gymnast they had on their back and how they figured it out. I've never seen these girls so talkative.

"Okay girls, time for dessert!" Savannah's mom announces, coming in with a tray of cupcakes. Savannah passes out plates and napkins and the girls are not shy selecting a cupcake.

We are quiet for a brief moment while everyone eats their treat.

"How is your flyaway Alexis?" Marissa asks, breaking the silence.

"I think I'll be ready by the intersquad. I'm doing it on the competition set onto an 8-incher. I think I'll be landing them on the 4-incher soon."

"They are so pretty," Lucy adds.

"What about you Lucy?" Marissa continues, "How are your back handsprings?" We all know Lucy has been struggling with her back handspring on beam since she had to change which hand she puts in front.

"It finally doesn't feel funny and my landing is getting consistent. I'm not sure if I'll do it in the intersquad, but I know I'll be able to do it this season."

"So you're doing them on high beam?" Trista asks.

"Yes, with 8-inchers," Lucy explains.

"Only two," Savannah interjects.

"How's it going for you, Paige?" I'm silent for a moment. My flyaway is the same, my tumbling is the same, and my vault is the same. "I'm adding a handstand to my back extension roll," I share, finally landing on something new that I'm doing.

"That sounds hard," Carmen says, and I smile at her. Marissa continues to ask the girls gymnastics questions to keep our conversation going. As I listen, I realize two things. One, my teammates are ready for the intersquad.

New Challenges

And two, Marissa is the new leader of the Level 5s.

Chapter 26

For the next two weeks I work hard in the gym to get my new Level 6 skills. Unfortunately I am not very close. A week ago Katie pulled me aside and said I needed to be clear on my A and B routines. She told me to start running full routines with a tuck flyaway on bars and a back tuck and front tuck on floor. Then when I'm done with an assignment I can work my new skills and eventually run the new skills in my B routines. I agreed with her, what else could I do? The problem is that it has been taking me the entire rotation to complete the assignment with my A routines. I never actually get to my B routines, or even the skills in the B routines. The upside is that I have been doing my A routines well all week.

    I just finished my last workout before the Level 6/7 intersquad tomorrow. Katie has given us a pep talk about how we are ready. Now that I have routines and I'm doing basic skills in them, she is right. I am ready. Sadly, I have the easiest skills of all the girls on the team. I found the downside of optionals. Everyone can see it if you're behind. In compulsories we all had the same skills so it felt more even. You either had your skills and got to compete or you didn't. Tomorrow I will be competing with baby skills compared to my teammates.

    "Why so quiet, Pumpkin?" my mom asks.

    I turn and look at her in the drivers seat. I sigh, "My routines feel dumb."

    "Dumb? They look beautiful to me."

    "But they are simple Level 5 skills. I didn't learn anything new."

    "Were you expecting to in six weeks?" she asks.

    "Yes," I pout crossing my arms. "I'm training more hours. I have Katie coaching me. I have been coming in extra. I thought I would at least have my layout flyaway or my layout on floor. Something!"

    "You've been growing so much," my mom starts.

    "Don't finish that sentence. I'm tired of everyone telling me how big and fat I am!"

    "No one said fat!" my mom exclaims.

    "What are you saying then?"

    "That when you grow you have to learn to do your skills with that new height."

    "And weight!" I fire at her. As soon as the car comes to a stop in the garage I jump out and slam the door and run up to my room.

I plop on the bed and Snow Queen comes scrambling out from under the bed. "Sorry girl," I say, knowing I scared her. I slide off the bed and sit on the floor to be next to her. She looks at me with skepticism. "I didn't mean to wake you from your nap," I try again. She looks at me and decides to walk over to me. I reach out and pet her. I stroke her silky coat that is now gray and black along the back. She purrs and rolls back over, stands up, and walks into my lap. We sit in silence for a while. Well, I am silent, she is purring up a storm.

I hear a knock on my door and Snow Queen launches out of my lap as my mom peeks her head in. "Can I come in?" she asks. I nod and she walks all the way into my room and sits down on the ground next to me. We are silent for a minute. Then she says, "It concerns me that you think growing into a healthy woman means that you are fat."

I roll my eyes and lean my head back, "Mo-um."

"What? Help me understand. Because to me you are perfect."

"I'm just . . . just . . . not the same," I choke out.

"Of course you aren't. You aren't supposed to be the same. You are a thirteen-year-old girl becoming a woman."

"What if I don't want to be a woman?"

"We can't stop these things, Paige. It's life."

"I feel so heavy. So huge."

"I imagine a sport in flight like gymnastics you notice every change in your body. That doesn't mean there is anything wrong with your body. You are just changing."

"It feels wrong," I sulk.

"I am sure it feels weird and different." she says,

tucking a curly strand of hair behind my ear. "You should see how you look doing your floor routine. It's stunning."

"But I don't do anything in it!" I wail. "And I look gigantic!" I add.

"Gigantic? Compered to who? You look the same as your teammates."

"No I don't. Savannah, Lucy, and Alexis are tiny."

"Paige, Savannah, Lucy, and Alexis are fifth graders. They are eleven and you are thirteen. You can't compare. Look at girls your age, the Level 7s. You are exactly the same size."

"I guess I don't think of them as my teammates yet."

"Well they are. Even if you weren't their size, there is still nothing wrong with you. You are exactly the size you are supposed to be. You have to stop comparing, Paige. It's not healthy."

We are quiet for a moment. I know my mom is right. I can't seem to tell her. I feel stuck in my bad mood. I feel gross inside.

Snow Queen wanders over to my mom and gives her a little bump with her head as an invitation to pet her.

"Do you still think Snow Queen is cute?"

"Of course I do! What kind of question is that?" I exclaim.

"Even though she's bigger and no longer white?" she asks.

"Mom, don't be silly," I say picking up Snow Queen. "She's still my sweet kitten."

My mom leans over and kisses my head and says, "And you will always be my sweet pumpkin."

"I walked right into that one," I say to Snow Queen.

"You aren't fat," my mom says.

"I know."

"Good. I need you to know and remember. Be confident and stop comparing yourself to others."

"Okay," I say without looking up. I feel dumb. I know I'm not fat. I just hate talking about my new size.

"Do you want to invite Katherine and Abigail to the intersquad?" she asks me.

"I though Grace and Chloe were coming for winter break."

"They are driving out tomorrow, but they won't be able to make it in time for your intersquad."

That's too bad, I was hoping to have friends there who don't know gymnastics very well. I guess Katherine and Abigail won't know that my routines are lame and lacking hard skills.

"Why not?" I say. "Mom? Do you think I should have stayed in Level 5?" I ask.

My mom takes her time answering and finally says, "From what I can tell you are between the two levels. I don't think you would have been happy staying in Level 5 any more than you are in Level 6."

"Maybe gymnastics doesn't make me happy anymore?" I wonder out loud.

"Only you can answer that pumpkin. But I do think you should participate in the intrasquad before you make any big decisions."

She kisses me on the forehead again and stands up. She quietly leaves me and a disappointed Snow Queen who was loving the attention.

I stand up, scooping up Snow Queen with me. I climb

New Challenges

into bed and try to get Snow Queen to stay with me. She wiggles out of my grasp and jumps off the bed. I roll to my side and think about my options.

I could quit and do whatever it is Katherine and Abigail do after school. I could skip this season and just train skills all year. I could swallow my pride and compete. I've never been the best, so why is being the clear worst bothering me so much?

I reach for my phone and text Abigail and Katherine:

> Me:
>> Do you guys want to come to my intersquad tomorrow?
>
> Abigail:
>> What's an intersquad?
>
> Katheryn:
>> What time?
>
> Me:
>> 2 and it's a practice meet at Perfect Balance.
>
> Katherine:
>> I'm in if we can catch a ride.
>
> Abigail:
>> Can I bring Quinn ?
>
> Katherine:
>> What? Is it that serious that you are doing stuff outside of school?!
>
> Abigail:
>> I just told him I'd hang out tomorrow.
>
> Me:
>> It's fine. He may think it boring though.
>
> Abigail:
>> Doubt it, plus, hanging out is usually boring. This

will be better.

I close my eyes. Bringing middle school boys was more than I bargained for, but that's Abigail for you. Our text thread turns into a conversation about boys. I can't contribute much so I end up reading their banter until Katherine addresses me directly.

Katherine:
> Paige, my mom can take us if yours can bring us home.

"Mom! Can you bring Katherine and Abigail home tomorrow after the intersquad?" I yell.
I wait a moment and hear, "Yes!"

Me:
> She can bring you home.

Katherine:
> Awesome, can't wait!

I set my phone down and lay back on my bed. I guess if I'm quitting or moving to Level 5, I'm not doing it until I attempt Level 6 in an intersquad.

Chapter 27

Katie decided to have us come in Saturday afternoon for the intersquad so we would have the gym to ourselves. As I walk up to the viewing area, the gym seems almost eerie. It's usually bustling with kids, coaches, and parents. I walk through the quiet parent viewing area and into the optionals room and over to my locker. I take off my sweats, wad them up and stuff them in my locker. I take a deep breath and realize I'm nervous. I'm not nervous of the skills I'm going to be doing. They are all skills I have been doing for a while. I'm nervous because for the first time I'm doing my own unique routines. What if the other girls think my routines with Level 5 skills are silly?

New Challenges

Too late now a voice says to me. I sigh again, grateful no one else is in here. I grab my water bottle and head back downstairs.

I go into the training room and see a few of the girls are already here. Since the gym is empty they didn't bother going up to the lockers, they just dumped their bags inside the training room doors.

I quietly join them and sit down in my splits. It's all the upper optional girls, Levels 8, 9, and 10. I don't know these girls well, but since we have the same competition season, we are doing our intersquad together. I'm excited to watch their routines and am intimidated for them to watch mine.

"Good morning, ladies," I hear James say as he walks up. I'm relieved to see James here.

"Are you coaching optionals this season?" I ask hopefully.

"There are a lot of you this morning, so Katie asked for me to help out," he explains.

"What events?" Kayla asks.

"Bars and Floor. Who needs a spot in their routine and which passes?" he asks. I listen as the girls tell him which pass they would like a spot on, double backs mostly.

"What about you, Paige?" he asks me. "Do you need help with your first pass?" he asks, referring to my back tuck. Or maybe he thinks I'm doing a layout. I should be by now.

"No, I'm just doing the tuck," I answer.

He nods and surveys the group. Most of the girls have arrived by now. "Ten laps ladies, then come back and stretch."

We stand up and start to run around the floor. This is a big group when you add in the upper optional girls. I look up at the parent viewing area as I run and I see it has filled in with parents who have come to watch.

We finish running and one of the Level 10s leads us in an organized stretching routine. We take up the entire floor and it is fun to be part of such a big group. When we are done we break into five lines and do a quick and basic complex that is, again, led by the Level 10s. When we're finished we go over to Katie to be told what events we are starting on.

"Thanks for warming us up Kayla. Girls, this is Jill and this is Sarah, they will be judging you today." My stomach sinks as I realize we have actual judges here. "They are going to help us make sure we have all the requirements in each routine and tell us what we need to work on. Upper optionals start on vault, lower optionals start on bars. 6s and 7s, go grip up," she tells us.

We walk over to the doors of the training area to get our grips. Some girls left their gym bags by the entrance of the training areas, some in the cubbies in the lobby, and some put their bags upstairs like a regular practice day.

Lucy and Alexis follow me upstairs, I assume their grips are in their lockers too.

"Are you nervous?" Alexis asks Lucy.

"Not as much as I thought I would be," Lucy tells her.

"You just seem quiet, but then again, you're a quiet person," Alexis observes.

"I'm glad to start on bars," I say, as we reach the top of the stairs. When we see all the parents in the training area our conversation stops and we walk quietly to the optionals

New Challenges

room.

We can hear the moms murmuring about warm-ups and what skills their daughters will be doing. Well, the moms that know the names of the skills. Savannah's mom knows stuff like that, my mom doesn't.

We walk into the optional room and over to our lockers. "Should we just grab our bags and take them downstairs since no one else is here today?" Lucy asks.

"Might as well," I agree. We grab our bags and head downstairs where we sit with the rest of our team by bars to put our grips on. We watch as James moves mats around and prepares for our bars rotation. He is talking to the judge, Jill, while he moves mats. Then he gets her a spotting block to sit on. Once he has her settled with a clipboard and a water, he turns to us, "Push away kips!" he yells.

We get in two lines at the competition bars for push away kips to warm up. Once we are done with kips we each do a first half, second half, and full set.

My tuck flyaways are consistent and I am finally comfortable doing them out of a cast. I'm just embarrassed I'm the only one doing a tuck flyaway. Savannah, Alexis, and Lucy all have their layout flyaway. I go over to the chalk tray. There is nothing I can do about it now except to do the best routine I can.

Once we've all done a full set James tells us our order and gives a piece of paper to Jill. I can see it has a grid with our names on it. I assume it's to keep track of our scores rather than using score cards like she would in a meet.

"Level 7s are going to start us off. Sixes, you can sit down," James tells us.

We walk over to the panel mat that James set out and we sit down facing the bars. I sit down, loosen my grips, and watch the girls on the Level 7 team learn their order. They are standing around the chalk tray quietly talking to James. While I wait for them to get situated I look up to see if my family has arrived on time.

I find my mom and wave. I spot Abigail and Katherine next to her. I notice no Quinn; probably for the best. I wonder what they are going to think of all this. At the very least they should have fun watching the Level 10s. As I'm scanning the parent viewing area I spot Trista, Carmen, and Marissa.

"Our 5s are here," I whisper to Alexis.

Alexis, looks up and waves to the girls and says, "That was nice." I smile to myself; it was.

We watch as Brooklyn steps over to the low bar, salutes our judge and begins. As soon as Brooklyn lands I hear girls cheering over at vault. I turn over my shoulder just in time to see one of the 10s do a beautiful layout Tsuk.

I look up to see if Abigail and Katheryn saw her and I see they are busy talking and completely missed it. I shake my head, maybe they won't be impressed by the 10s. Trista and Carmen are clapping furiously, I know *they* appreciated that vault.

I turn back to watch Aubrey take her turn. Aubrey and the rest of the 7s do clean routines that swing just a little higher than ours. When they're finished they take their seat on our panel mat and we get up and go to the chalk tray.

James comes over to us and gives us our order. He has me go first, then Savannah, Alexis, Lucy, Riley, and Victoria. I do a quick kip clear hip for my one-touch and

New Challenges

then chalk up and wait to compete. I stand by the low bar and watch my teammates finish their one touch.

James sets out the springboard for my mount and comes over to me. "Swing tight and clean. Get those shoulders in front on your casts," he says. "I've seen them get pretty high lately," he says, making me smile. My casts have gotten higher. They aren't to handstand yet, but they are above the required 45-degree angle.

He steps away from me and immediately the judge salutes me. I salute back and step up onto the springboard. I take a deep breath and jump into my glide kip. I cast above 45 degrees and go right into a decent clear hip circle, then I swing down into another kip. I pike on, jump to the high bar, kip, cast. The cast feels big, I swing down and right into my tuck flyaway. I let go at just the right time and, to my surprise, I stick the landing.

I turn to the judge and salute that I am done. She gives me a nice smile and looks down at her notes. James comes up to me with a big high five. "That was nice and clean. You'll score well," he says. I will? But I didn't really do anything. I walk over to the panel mat, tugging off my grips as I walk. When I sit down, the 7s congratulate me on a good routine.

We are using an old-school scoring stand. The judge is putting up the scores herself before she turns to the next routine. She flips up a score and then turns the stand for me to see. An 8.5. Wait, what? I look at her to catch her eye to see if that score is meant for me, but the judge is already saluting Savannah.

How did I get an 8.5? I didn't do anything. I don't go to handstand on my casts or clear hips, and I did a tuck flyaway. Maybe she meant 7.5. I can ask James after the meet. I watch as Savannah jumps to the high bar, casts to handstand, and does a big layout flyaway. She is arched in the air and she takes several big steps on the landing, but at least she did the layout.

She gets a high five from James and comes over to sit with us. I give her a side hug as she sits down. "You're getting pretty good at bars Anna," I say.

She smiles, "It's fun," she says as she peels off her grips. We watch as the judge turns Savannah's score toward us, 7.70. That can't be right. Thankfully Savannah doesn't ask me what I got and we go straight to watching Alexis.

The rest of our rotation moves quickly since bars is a fast event and we only have one judge to wait for. The upper optionals have come over from vault and are putting on their grips as they watch Victoria, our last routine.

When Victoria is done we walk over to vault. Our judge, Jill, comes with us. The judges will talk to us about our routines at the end of the meet. Therefore, we need the same judge watching us for all four events.

We work with Katie to set up vault. The upper optionals vault with only 8-inch and 4-inch mats behind the vaulting table. We vault with huge mats behind the vaulting table so we need to set them up.

We help Katie push the port-a-pit in place behind the table. Then we throw two more 8-inchers on top. When we are done setting up we run back down the runway for a quick sprint warm-up and then we each do two vaults.

Katie tells us our order and this time we are sorted by the type of timer we do rather than Level 6 and 7. The girls

New Challenges

doing Yurchenko entries are first. Katie wraps the springboard with the yellow square mat made to go around the board. Then she stands partially on it as she waits for her first Yurchenko vaulter to go.

Lucy is the only Level 6 doing the Yurchenko entry. I think she practiced it more at her last gym before she came to Perfect Balance. Alexis is doing a front handspring entry and Savannah, Maya, Brooklyn and I are doing Tsuk entries. The five of us sit on floor and watch our teammates.

They all seem to score in the same 8.0 to 8.8 range. Then it's our turn. Their vaults go so fast that Katie says we don't need a one touch vault. We line up in the order Katie tells us and we are ready.

I am to go after Maya and Brooklyn, which is intimidating because I'm sure their form is better than mine.

Both Maya and Brooklyn do clean half-ons and it's my turn. Vault gives me no jitters. It has always been easier for me and this is one area where my new height and weight seem to help. I salute the judge and step onto the runway. I run, hurdle, and punch. I think of twisting in my shoulders while driving my heels like Katie and James have taught me. I do a half turn up onto the table and try to block and pop to my feet on the mats behind the table. I try to keep my momentum moving and fall to my back after my feet hit. The fall at the end seems forced, but hopefully the judge didn't notice. Falling is part of the skill that helps us rotate. Eventually we will do a flip to our feet without the mats behind the table. I stand up and salute Judge Jill.

When I climb down Katie is there to walk down the

runway with me for my second one. "Good form and drive on the front half. Keep that momentum on the back half. Think of rotating to your back rather the landing on your feet and falling back," she says. So much for no one noticing.

I nod and stop at my spot on the runway. Katie gives my shoulder a squeeze and steps away from me. I turn and the judge is still looking down calculating my score. Then she looks up at me. She sees I am looking at her so she salutes and I salute back. I step onto the runway.

Keep moving I think to myself. I run and do a vault basically the same as the first one. So much for keep moving. It's harder than it sounds.

Katie greets me with high fives and goes to Savannah to talk with her before her vault. I have no idea what kind of score I'll get on vault and I'm pleased with a simple 8.0. I look up at my mom and friends in the parent viewing area and I'm glad they came. It makes it more like a meet.

After the rest of my team finishes their vaults we rotate to floor and the upper optionals go to beam. We know to go to different corners and to start tumbling on the diagonal. James is with us on floor and Katie went to beam. I'm glad he is here because I know he'll step in on my back tuck if I don't set well.

James doesn't time us like in a meet but just tells us to do one good version of each tumbling pass. I do my front tucks first. It only takes me two tries to feel good. Then I go on to my round-off back handspring back tuck. They feel okay today. Not as sluggish as they have been in the past. Maybe it's the extra adrenaline or maybe I'm finally getting used to my new height. Whatever the reason, I'm

New Challenges

glad it feels okay.

I walk over to James when I'm done. "Are you done warming up the tumbling?" He asks me and I nod that I am. "Then warm up your leap and turn along the edge while you wait for the rest of your team to finish."

I do my leap pass along the edge of the floor. By the time the rest of the girls are done I'm more than ready to compete floor. I'm excited to do floor today; even my lame tumbling can't diminish my excitement to perform my very own floor routine.

I look up to the viewing area and I see my dad and brother have joined my mom and my friends. They came straight from Jason's indoor soccer practice. I'm glad they didn't miss floor.

James gathers us together and gives us our order. I notice he has the 6s going first and then the 7s. We sit down along the floor and Alexis starts us off. She has a pretty routine performed to a Beauty and the Beast medley. Alexis is clean and precise and I can tell she is getting more comfortable with her routine. She does a clean layout on her first pass and a front handspring dive roll for her second pass.

Next up is Savannah, who also has her layout and front handspring dive roll. Savannah is performing a peppy and fun routine to the Zombie's movie music. She looks like she is having fun on floor, which makes up for her less than perfect dance lines. Then Lucy is up and I start getting nervous. Why would James have me go after Lucy? She is so good. Her tumbling is amazing and her dance is fun and engaging. As Lucy does a perfect layout I begin to get nervous. Then I watch her dance to her music from the movie Home with an energy I cannot imagine having on floor. My team starts clapping to her music and I look around at everyone enjoying her routine. I stand up to get my blood moving and watch Lucy prepare for her second pass. I walk to my corner as I watch her do a beautiful front handspring front tuck.

Tough act to follow.

I get to the edge of the floor as she is walking off and I give her a high five. "Great routine," I say, and I mean it.

James greets Lucy and murmurs something to her before coming over to me. "You ready?" he asks me.

"My dance is. My tumbling is questionable," I admit.

"You are doing perfectly acceptable Level 6 passes. Own it and show off your dance."

Since I don't really know what is acceptable for Level 6, I don't argue with him. All I know is that all of my teammates do harder skills. He pats my back and moves away from me so Jill can see that I'm ready. There's not much I can do about my tumbling now. All I can do is show off my pretty new floor routine and hope my friends and parents like it.

Judge Jill salutes me, I salute back and walk onto the floor. It's nice and comfortable to do a routine in our own gym. I feel only mildly nervous as I take my starting position. My music starts and I do my dance into the corner, take a deep breath, and run for my first tumbling pass. I do a typical round-off back handspring back tuck. Typical is good considering all of my challenges lately. When I land I am so happy to have done a nice high back tuck. Even more surprising is how my teammates are cheering for me. They know how hard these last several weeks have been for me. I smile and keep going. I enjoy the music and dance of a routine that fits me far better than compulsories ever did. I do my leap pass, dance, pose in the corner and I pause for a moment before my second and final pass of a simple front tuck. I run, punch, and do a clean front tuck with a stuck landing. I do my brief dance sequence and prepare for a one and a half turn. I'm proud of this because most Level 6s do just a full turn. I complete a perfect one and a half turn, dance, do my jump combination and hit my ending pose. I salute the judge and walk off the floor.

My teammates give me high fives and Lucy says, "I think that's the prettiest routine I have even seen."

"Thanks Lucy," I say sitting down next to her.

James walks over and gives me a quick high five and says, "Great crowd pleaser," and then turns to Riley who is next.

I turn and watch the judge intently. I have no idea what to expect. My tumbling is so basic, it could be bad. She adjusts the numbers, turns the stand to us, and then salutes Riley. I can hear my teammates cheering for Riley as she begins, but I'm too shocked to join in. The stand says 8.85. That doesn't seem possible. There is nothing in my routine. Savannah and Lucy got a point lower than me and they were doing way harder stuff. I look up at my mom and she silently claps for me when I catch her eye. I wave at her and my friends and turn back to Riley. I'm not sure how I got that score. I don't think I deserved it. Katie said the judges are going to go over our routines and scores for us at the end of the intrasquad. I'm interested to see what she says.

We enjoy watching the 7s compete on floor and then we head to beam. The upper optionals are not done with beam yet, so we warm-up on the two beams farthest away from the beam they are competing on. We make sure to warm up as quietly as possible. I do each of the skills in my routine once, a dance through, and I'm ready.

I finish slightly before my teammates so I stand next to James and watch the Level 10s compete. They are so good. I can't imagine doing a back handspring on beam, much less three in a row. I look up at my family and friends in the viewing area and they are riveted. I'm glad the 10s are here to make the intrasquad more interesting for everyone who came today.

The last girl competing beam dismounts. The upper optional girls talk to Katie for a moment and then walk over to James.

"You guys ready to end strong?" he asks them. They all answer something different at once making him laugh as they walk over to floor together.

Katie comes over to us, "How was floor?"

We are silent for a moment and finally Maya says, "We all hit, so it might be time for B routines already." The girls laugh and I notice they are good natured about skills they haven't gotten yet.

"Alright, how about a one touch on the competition beam and we'll begin." We walk over to the far beam and each take a quick turn in the order we're going to compete. I'm third up, which is perfect in my opinion. I can rest after my one-touch and get my head together, but I also don't have to wait too long.

I watch Brooklyn and Maya start us off. They each fall

on their series. At least they're doing a series. Now it's my turn to do my puny routine that has no back walkover and no back handspring. *You have a skill no one else can do* my little voice reminds me. That's true, no one else can do a back extension roll on beam. I stand by the beam as Katie walks up.

"Enjoy it up there. You have a clean routine, show Jill that."

"Thank you," I say. She smiles at me and moves away.

Judge Jill salutes and I salute back. I do my simple mount of splits and stand up. I do a nice leap pass, pose and then I kick into a nice tight handstand. I step down and try to do my back extension roll as quickly as possible. I make the back extension roll, but it was definitely not connected to the handstand. I have never connected it so I didn't really intend to. Happy to have made the back extension roll I do a pose, my full turn, and cross steps to move me to the end of the beam. Then I do a clean cartwheel, my jumps, and turn to do my dismount going the other way. My dismount is a simple front tuck and I land it well.

I turn and salute the judge with a big grin. I stayed on! That's something to be proud of.

Katie comes over and give me a high five, "Beautiful. You are going to be a fun beam worker to train over the years." I dip my head, surprised at her compliment.

I go over and sit next to my teammates. They all congratulate me for staying on and then they turn to Alexis, who is next. Alexis has to wait for the judge to figure out my score before she can go, and it is an unusually long wait. Finally, she stops writing, takes the score stand, fiddles with the numbers, and turns it toward us. She is saluting Alexis I see my score. 9.15. What? That can't be right. I look around in confusion. I want to be excited about my scores, I just can't let myself be excited because I don't believe they are right. What is going on?

I look up at my old teammates in the parent viewing area. Marissa gets my attention and holds up a piece of paper with says 33.85 in big black letters. Then she gives me a thumbs up.

Is that right? A 33.85? Did I really just get one of my best all-around scores in a Level 6 intrasquad? James always said I would do well in optionals. Can I believe these scores? I look up at Trista, Marissa, and Carmen. They seem to believe it.

I watch as almost all of my teammates fall on beam doing their new skills. I guess that's what an intersquad is for, to try new skills and get the jitters out.

When our group is done on beam, floor is not even half way done. The upper optionals have longer routines than ours by almost double. I'm glad they aren't done because I love watching them. We sit along the edge of the floor to watch the show.

I see Katie and Judge Jill talking out of the corner of my eye. I'm sure she has a lot to say about us and I'm dying to hear what it is. I sigh; she will talk to us as soon as the upper optional girls are done with floor.

I watch Kayla, a Level 10, salute the judge and start her routine. Kayla has grown since I've been watching her in the gym these last few years. In fact, she is kind of tall. I watch her open with a beautiful piked double back. She smiles bright as she runs into a complicated leap pass. Kayla is like the college girls on the poster Katie showed me. She has broad shoulders, a chest, and muscled arms and legs. She is bigger than me, and yet, I think she is gorgeous. I look at Alexis sitting next to me. Maybe I do need to stop comparing myself to younger girls. I'm growing into a gymnast like Kayla.

    I look up at my friends and family again and see they are engrossed in the floor routine going on. I smile to myself; I can't blame them. These girls are inspiring. I relax and try to enjoy the last three routines.

Chapter 28

As soon as the upper optional girls are done competing in our intersquad, the judges gather us around them in two groups. The upper optionals sit down in the middle of the floor with Katie and we are ushered to sit over by beam to listen to Judge Jill with James.

"Great meet today! I would say you are all ready for a successful optionals season. Your coaches have asked me to go over each event and tell you where I took deductions. We will go in Olympic order. Vault was solid over all. Most of my deductions came from the body position off the table."

She continues to tell us how vault judging works. I

learn that most of my deductions were from not blocking off the table. Then she moves on to bars.

"In Level 6 your casts need to be above 45 degrees. All of you did that and some of you even went to handstand. I love seeing the handstands but the girls that went to handstand had major form breaks, causing a lot of deductions." Then she points to me, "Paige, is it?" I nod nervously. "Paige has all of her casts above 45 degrees and she had no form breaks in her cast, so she had less deductions than someone who maybe went all the way to handstand."

She continues talking about the requirements in Level 6 and I learn that my tuck flyaway is worth the same as a layout flyaway. I did not get a deduction for doing the easier dismount. My scores are starting to make sense.

Judge Jill moves on to beam. She talks about the basic requirements and deductions. Then she turns to me again, "Are you planning to connect the handstand to the back extension roll?"

"Yes," I say, even though I'm not sure if I'll ever get it.

"Good. You're getting a deduction for not having a connected series or a flight element." I nod, this is not news to me. I know I need to have one or the other. "Your leaps are almost 180 degrees and your turn is very controlled. I had very few deductions for you other than that requirement."

Then she turns to Lucy and gives her specific feedback on the requirements in her routine. I don't exactly hear what she's saying because I am shocked and pleased that the score she gave me is what she meant. I really did earn a

9.15 on beam.

After a long discussion with the Level 7s on their beam scores she finally moves to floor. She addresses us, the Level 6s, first.

"All of you met the requirements. Most of your deductions came from leaps, jumps, and turns. Spend time on your dance, it will vastly improve your score." Then she talks to a few of the girls about some big deductions on leaps that can be easily corrected.

"My favorite routine of the day was Swan Lake," she says turning to me. "It was clean with beautiful extension and lines. You were a joy to watch. That routine should score well for you all season."

"Thank you," I squeak out. *Favorite routine of the day?*

"I know we put a lot of value on the tumbling and you guys are trying to reach goals and move to the next level. But remember, to a judge, the tumbling is only half the routine. You must work on all of it."

She talks a little more to specific girls. All I can hear is *favorite routine of the day* over and over in my head. Here I thought I was going to be the scrub of the day. The lowest scorer, the girl who should consider sitting out of the Level 6 season.

"Thank you for your insight," James says. "We'll get working on everything you shared with us as soon as they come in on Monday." Then he turns to us, "Ladies you are free to go. If you want a print out of your scores, come to my office in five minutes and I will have them for you."

Immediately girls pop up and start talking, heading to their gym bags, and finding their parents. Parents have come down from the viewing area and are talking with kids in the lobby. I walk out into the lobby and find my parents and friends.

"I don't know what you were worried about," Katherine says, throwing her hair over her shoulder. "You were, like, one of the best ones on your team."

I laugh at her comment and say, "I don't know about that, but apparently my routines score well."

"Great job today pumpkin," my mom says, giving me a hug.

"Thanks Mom," I say, hugging her back. I turn to my friends and thank them for coming.

Katherine was right, I don't know what I was worried about. So I grew. So what? I can still do Level 6; and do it well. My routines aren't what I thought they would be, but they still score well. My body is not what I want it to be, but I noticed today that I look like the upper optional girls. I still look like a gymnast, just an older gymnast.

Maybe my mind has it all wrong and I need to just enjoy gymnastics and not try to be like anyone else.

"I really liked that backwards roll to handstand thing you did on beam," Abigail says. "No one else did that."

I smile, "No one else does. My gymnastics is a little different."

"I like it," she says.

"So do I."

About the Author

Melisa Torres is the best-selling author of the Perfect Balance Gymnastics Series. She grew up in San Jose, California where she trained at Almaden Valley Gymnastics Club and competed in USA Gymnastics' Junior Olympic program for ten years. Melisa then attended Utah State University where she studied Psychology and Literature and competed for their NCAA Division 1 Gymnastics Team. Melisa was a two-time Academic All-American and team captain.

Melisa currently lives in Utah and is a single mother to two active boys. She enjoys attending their soccer games and taking them to the library. When Melisa is not parenting or writing she can be found weight lifting or partner dancing.

*Read the original
Perfect Balance Gymnastics Series!*

I've Got This!
Nothing Better Than Gym Friends
Dance is the Secret Event
Brothers Have Talent, Too
The Kip
Score Out
Courage to Fly
Season of Change

Perfect Balance Gymnastics Workbooks:
Goal Setting Journal
Overcoming Mental Blocks
Perfect Balance Gymnastics Coloring Book

PERFECT BALANCE GYMNASTICS SERIES
Grace and Confidence for Life!

MELISATORRES.COM
*For unique gymnastics gifts,
book signing dates, and to apply for our
Reader of the Month Program.*

FACEBOOK.COM/PBGSERIES
*For articles about gymnastics and
updates on new releases.*

@PERFECTBALANCEGYMBOOKS
*Following gymnasts and young writers to
give encouragement and inspiration*

Printed in Great Britain
by Amazon